small habits
big changes

How the Tiniest Steps Lead to a
Happier, Healthier You

Steven Handel

Ulysses Press

Published in the United States by:
Ulysses Press
P.O. Box 3440
Berkeley, CA 94703
www.ulyssespress.com

ISBN: 978-1-61243-831-3
Library of Congress Control Number: 2018944076

Printed in Canada by Marquis Book Printing
10 9 8 7 6 5 4 3 2

Acquisitions editor: Bridget Thoreson
Managing editor: Claire Chun
Editor: Phyllis Elving
Copyeditor: Barbara Schultz
Proofreader: Renee Rutledge
Front cover design: Justin Shirley
Cover and interior art: finger string © Martial Red/shutterstock.com
Production: Claire Sielaff

Distributed by Publishers Group West

small habits
big changes

Contents

Introduction

Every single choice you make influences your life in some way.

When your choices become ingrained in your daily routine, they end up becoming habits that are hard to change. Our daily choices become a deep part of how we see ourselves and how we live our lives.

We don't always realize the power behind these choices, because they start off being small and inconsequential. They only grow into something larger and more significant over time. One day you try your first cup of coffee, for whatever reason. Maybe a friend offers it to you, or you've watched your parents drink coffee for years, or you feel the need for a boost of energy before school or work. The initial reason doesn't really matter. Now fast-forward 10 or 20 years, and drinking that cup of coffee is likely *something you do without thinking*. It's just a normal part of your morning routine—and you don't even question it.

Every habit follows a similar pattern. Every habit starts off with a conscious decision (even if it's just "Hmm, I'll try that!"), then transforms into something you do because it has become a part of who you are. It's not conscious. It doesn't need a reason. You drink coffee every morning because you drink coffee every morning. That's it.

All habits eventually become self-fulfilling behaviors in this way. That's why they can be so powerful and so difficult to change. Of course, a habit can be healthy and constructive (such as going to the gym, reading books, or eating healthy foods), or a habit can be unhealthy and destructive (smoking cigarettes, arguing with people, or eating junk food).

Healthy or unhealthy, habits define our lives. They also determine where we are going in life and what waits in our future. Show me a person's daily routine and I'll tell you where they are heading in their future life. No, not because I'm psychic, but because our habits always have long-term consequences, positive or negative.

Habits are influential, but they aren't destiny. We have the power to change our habits if we are armed with the right mindset and tools to help us create long-lasting change in our lives. That's the goal behind this book: to equip you with the information and techniques to make changing habits simple, easy, and fun.

My approach is focused on making *tiny* changes.

Why You Need to Think Smaller

When people think about "self-improvement," they may imagine big changes happening in their lives overnight. People who have never hit the gym before or seen a vegetable on their plate start setting unrealistic goals—"I'm going to start going to the gym seven days a week and only eat kale!"

But how likely is it that they are going to be able to stick with their new goals?

Often when people try making big changes quickly, they soon become stressed, frustrated, and burnt out. Then they snap back to their old patterns. This is exactly why so many people who try to lose weight by following a special diet have a tough time keeping the weight off. They see their diet as a quick, temporary solution to a problem, without understanding the importance of thinking about the longer term.

I call this book *Small Habits, Big Changes* because I believe the key to self-improvement isn't to think bigger, but to think *smaller*. This means finding small habits that can build up exponentially over time.

Change rarely happens in one big moment. Change is often slow and gradual.

People fail at so many of their goals because they can't think small and long-term. They get caught trying to find that one magical solution that will change everything. And then when it doesn't, they give up on self-improvement entirely. If you've ever given up on a goal, it's likely because you weren't thinking *small* enough and thus went back to your former habits when you weren't able to make the big change you wanted.

Let's say one of the things you want to change is your diet. You could completely overhaul your current diet: throw out everything in your kitchen and go shopping for "healthy" foods that you've never eaten before. Or you could start much smaller. Maybe instead of trying to change yourself completely overnight, you focus on a tiny change, such as one of these:

- Substitute water for all of your soda intake.

- Change your midday snack from potato chips to fruit or a salad.

- Stop eating that candy bar while watching TV at night.

These are small habits that make a great starting point for healthier eating.

There are good reasons why focusing on tiny changes is way more effective than focusing on instant big changes. First, it's easier to make a tiny change. It takes less willpower and less energy, so it's more achievable. Second, accomplishing that tiny change will buoy up your confidence and prove to you that change is indeed possible.

Finally, success in making a tiny change starts to change the way you think about yourself. Once that change becomes a consistent habit, you've begun to change your identity and how you see yourself. Now you're no longer that person who drinks soda at every meal, eats potato chips every day, or eats candy while watching TV. Now you're the person who drinks water with every meal, snacks on a healthy salad, or can sit and watch TV without needing something sweet in your mouth.

When that tiny change influences you to see yourself in a new way, it opens up new opportunities for change. You start thinking, "Hey, I stopped drinking soda, so why can't I stop eating junk food, too?" Gradually you begin to see yourself as a healthy person who does healthy things. That's just who you are now.

You'll be surprised by how much you can change in your life through nothing but tiny, gradual changes. Throughout this book, you'll find collections of small habits to consider adding to your daily routine, along with tips and tools to try. Think of these as the nuts and bolts you can use to build up your daily routine, the tiniest of actions you can do each day to promote growth and well-being. But consider these to be *suggestions*—you don't have to do all of them, but I want you to have many options from which to choose.

One big theme behind all self-improvement is that it requires self-experimentation. You'll find that some advice works for you and some doesn't make any sense whatsoever. That's completely fine. Different things work for different people. Most importantly, be willing to try new things, because that's the only way to discover what works best for you.

Get excited about pushing your boundaries a bit. Slowly. Each day. Just a little bit.

Taking Action vs. Being an Information Junkie

One of the biggest traps in self-improvement effort is becoming an "information junkie."

An information junkie is someone who spends a lot of time reading books, watching videos, and listening to podcasts about self-improvement but spends little time putting what they learn into practice. This is a common problem. We stuff our brains with information, then find ourselves not knowing what to do with it. This is especially true in our current age, where we are constantly consuming information on the internet and through social media.

Of course, it's a positive thing to want to learn as much as possible and to do your own research into various topics. Even the occasional surfing on Google and Wikipedia can be fun and informative. Clearly, if I believed that learning new things was pointless, I wouldn't bother writing this book. But there comes a point when, if you're not able to apply information to your everyday life, you have to ask: How useful is it, really? Endlessly seeking new information can become a distraction. We feel we're not quite ready to make a change, so we think, "Well, I should really read more about this before I decide what the best course of action is!"

But this can become a never-ending task. You'll never know *everything* about a topic. Being successful at reaching your goals means learning how to take action, even when you realize you don't have complete knowledge.

Even more importantly, much of what we learn throughout our lives comes not from books or videos, but through personal experience and trying new things. By focusing on information and not action, you're actually *limiting* your education and self-growth by ignoring the importance of hands-on experience. It's like reading books about how to play baseball without ever picking up a ball, or watching videos of people riding a bicycle without ever getting on a bike. How good can you really get without any experience? When we fall into the trap of becoming an information junkie, we spend too much time "learning" and not enough time "doing."

This brings us back to the main theme of this book: small habits and tiny changes. Tiny changes are tiny actions. This is how we begin transforming "information ⟶ action"—by thinking small and identifying the things we can start doing *today* to change the way we live our lives.

Be Patient with Yourself

It's essential to approach self-improvement with the right attitude. Before you start putting any of the advice in this book into action, I want to make sure that you approach this whole self-improvement endeavor with the right intentions and expectations.

First, I want to highlight the importance of having *patience*.

Our patience is strongest when we have a healthy expectation of future difficulties and obstacles. Get ready to be challenged. Get ready to make mistakes. Get ready to fail. And make sure you are ready to keep *moving forward* no matter what happens.

While this book aims to make self-change as effortless as possible, it's unrealistic to expect that you won't experience a bit of frustration and failure. I'm saying this because I want you to be prepared. Patience comes with accepting that struggles and hardships are a part of life, and it thereby prepares us to face these struggles and hardships when they actually happen.

No matter where you are in life, you're never going to reach a point at which all your troubles magically go away. New obstacles will always present themselves. Therefore, the best attitude to have isn't to ignore these future obstacles or try to live your life avoiding them, but to be ready to accept and even embrace them.

What's amazing and powerful is that the more you accept the possibility of future obstacles in your life, the less intense and dramatic they seem when they actually happen. With patience, negative events seem less surprising or shocking. And this allows you to respond in a more grounded, calm, and understanding way.

Be patient with your life. And be patient with yourself.

Don't beat yourself up over your mistakes. Don't give up at the first sight of failure. Instead, have a healthy expectation that you *will* make mistakes every now and then. And you *will* fail every now and then. Why? Because it's true. There will always be ups and downs—and they are part of the process.

Believe it or not, patience is an important part of healthy self-esteem. Patience is about setting realistic standards and goals for yourself, and not drowning in the hope of achieving the impossible goal of perfection. If you think you have to be perfect in order to feel good about yourself, then you will never feel good about yourself.

Now let's get started!

CHAPTER ONE
Your Daily Routine

What you do on a daily basis is what creates the life you live.

We tend to take our daily activities for granted. They become a routine that we repeat over and over again without thinking about it, and we rarely take the time to think about our daily patterns and how they might be influencing us.

But your daily routine is ultimately what influences where you're going in your life and what the future holds for you. So, when you think about "changing your life," what you should really be thinking about is "changing your routine."

Before you focus on making any changes, however, I suggest doing a bit of introspection. The goal is to write out what a typical day in your life looks like. This simple exercise will help you reflect on your current daily routine and identify areas where you might want to start making changes.

This should take no more than 10 to 15 minutes. Don't overthink it—you're not being graded. This is just an opportunity to step back and reflect for a bit.

# exercise
List All Your Daily Activities

STEP **1.** Take a piece of paper and a pen (or open up a text document on your computer) and write "My Daily Routine" as the title of your document.

STEP **2.** Start from the very beginning of your day. The first item on your list will be "Wake up."

STEP **3.** Write down everything you do during the day, roughly in the order in which you do it. For example, the next items may be "Make my bed," "Go to the bathroom," "Take a shower," "Get dressed," and so on. The order doesn't have to be perfect—we all have variations from day to day—but try to come up with a rough outline of your average day, from start to finish.

STEP **4.** Repeat activities that you do more than once a day (such as "Eating"). It's repetitive, but it will make your outline more accurate and give you a more complete picture.

STEP **5.** You can include regular weekly activities as well ("Grocery shopping," "Laundry," "Cleaning"). You don't need to list everything or fill up every hour, but leave room and flexibility for things you do frequently though not necessarily every day.

STEP **6.** For the end of your day, the last item on your list should be "Go to sleep."

STEP **7.** Once you've completed your timeline, go back and categorize each activity based on what area of your life it influences. If you feel an activity fulfills multiple areas, go ahead and list it in more than one category. These might be some of your categories:

- Health

- Work/chores

- Leisure

- Family/friends

- Personal/spiritual

STEP **8.** Now go back and mark each activity according to the type of influence you think it has on your life:

- Positive

- Negative

- Neutral

STEP **9.** Decide if each activity is something you need to do more of (+), less of (-), or about the same as you're doing now (=), and mark accordingly.

STEP **10.** Review your complete routine and think of one to three activities that aren't listed but that you'd like to do more often. List them below your routine and mark "+" next to them.

STEP **11.** Save your document in a folder labeled "Self-Improvement."

Now ask yourself this question: "Is this the type of routine I could follow every day until I die?" This can bring insight, because your goal is to develop a sustainable, long-term routine. If you find it difficult to imagine living like this, over and over, forever (or for an extended period of time), that could be a sign that you need to make some changes. Your current path is unsustainable.

There will always be changes and variations from day to day. We don't want every single day to be exactly the same, or to have to follow the same routine like a mindless robot. That's not the goal of developing a routine.

Nothing about your daily routine is set in stone. The point is to begin thinking in a long-term way about the things you are doing each day, and how they are influencing your life. Remember—even the smallest actions, done over a long period of time, can build up into something huge. A couple of cigarettes in a day won't kill you, but if you follow that pattern long enough you are setting yourself up for major consequences. Likewise, going to the gym once won't change your health or appearance, but going to the gym consistently for a year will make a noticeable difference.

This principle is true for almost every habit we have. Often it's not any single act that will completely change your life, but the consistency and the persistence of a habit that leads to real consequences over time. That's why paying attention to your daily routine is essential for self-growth and self-improvement.

Plan to come back to this exercise every now and then to get a sense of how you are spending your time each and every day. This awareness is a first step toward making positive life changes.

CHAPTER TWO

The Basics: Sleep, Diet, and Exercise

How we take care of our bodies and our physical health is one of the most significant factors when it comes to maximizing our days and reaching our full potential. There are three basic elements that have to do with our overall physical health: sleep, diet, and exercise.

We all sleep, eat, and exercise (or don't exercise) daily. But these activities are so basic to us that we almost take them for granted, forgetting just how important they are—even though they can have a huge influence on our lives. All of these activities can have a spillover effect on your day, influencing your mental focus, energy level, and stamina.

Simply put, your health ties into almost every other aspect of your life. That is likely why health-related goals are among the most common when it comes to self-improvement—and rightfully so. If you don't get enough sleep one night, that can ruin your day. We've all been there: It makes us less motivated and less focused at work, more moody and irritable around others. It hurts our ability to make the most of our day and be our best self.

We all want to look good, feel good, and live long and healthy lives. Often, we take our health for granted until we start to feel rotten, but it's important to focus on getting healthy sooner rather than later. As we dive deeper into our daily routines and how they influence our lives, let's begin to focus on these basics that define each and every person's life.

Sleep

Healthy sleep habits are essential to getting your life and daily routine in order. Without a good night's sleep we can suffer a variety of physical and mental issues, from fatigue to stress and distracted thinking. Over time, these can build up and contribute to bigger problems, such as depression and anxiety disorders.

Getting your sleep right can make a noticeable difference in your life. If you are experiencing difficulties with your sleep patterns, here are some key principles to consider.

Are You an Early Bird or a Night Owl?

Psychologists and biologists know that humans fall into two main categories when it comes to sleep. These are based on differences in our circadian rhythms, or biological clocks.

An early bird prefers to go to bed earlier and wake up earlier, while a night owl prefers to stay up later and wake up later. Early birds tend to feel most energized in the morning, and night owls feel most energized later in the day. Understanding your biological clock is important when adjusting your sleep schedule to meet your personal needs.

In general, 7 to 10 hours of sleep is what most humans need (with rare exceptions), but *when* you should get this sleep depends greatly on whether you're more of an early bird or a night owl. Sometimes we need to adapt our sleep hours according to when we need to get to work or school. But to determine the *optimal* time to go to bed, ask yourself this question: "Am I more of a morning person or a night person?"

Stay Consistent with Your Sleep Schedule

One of the best things you can do to develop healthy sleep patterns is to maintain a consistent schedule from day to day. You should be going to sleep and waking up at about the same time every day.

This is important to recognize, because many people spend a night or two each week staying up really late, then try to compensate by sleeping a lot the next day (usually on the weekend).

Constantly needing to catch up on your sleep hours can really throw off your biological clock and keep you from developing a steady sleep rhythm. Try your best to follow the same sleep routine each day.

You can use an alarm clock to help set your sleep schedule, but ideally when you've found your biological rhythm you will wake up naturally around the same time every day. That's not required, but it's a sign that you're attuned to your body's needs.

Use Your Bedroom Just for Sleeping

If you spend a lot of time in your bedroom on activities that aren't related to sleeping (such as watching TV, playing video games, or doing homework), then your mind begins to associate that room with all those activities. One of the best things I've personally done is to get rid of the television and computer in my bedroom. Now that room is used almost solely for rest and sleeping. If I want to do something else, I have to go into another room.

This helps a lot, because our minds can be extremely sensitive to environmental cues (something we will discuss in a later chapter). Limiting the distractions in your bedroom helps you focus on sleep. Your mind begins to associate that room with sleeping. When you walk through the door and lay your head on the pillow, your mind is registering, "Now it's sleep time."

Be Physically Active during the Day

A good night's sleep often follows a good day's work. The more energy we exert while we are awake, the easier it is to fall asleep once the day comes to an end.

If you spend your days lazing around and being physically inactive, or even taking lots of naps, that's going to make it more difficult to fall asleep when it's actually time to get some rest. All the energy you don't use throughout the day can make you anxious and fidgety. Your body needs to engage in physical activity to release this energy.

Our lives are a cycle of work and rest, so you need to get the work part down in order to get the rest part down.

Minimize Alcohol and Drug Use

Alcohol and drugs can be a kind of sleep aid, but often they don't give you a healthy and productive sleep. They knock you out but don't give you the proper amount of REM sleep. It's not good to have a dependence on particular substances to manage your sleep cycle. Needing a drink every night to fall asleep, for example, could be a sign that you need to find healthier sleep habits.

Learn Relaxation Techniques

Learning relaxation techniques to practice before sleep is a better aid than alcohol or drugs. One of the most popular techniques is called "progressive muscle relaxation." In this simple exercise, you focus on the muscles in each part of your body, stretching and then releasing them while focusing on calmness in that specific area.

Start by focusing on your toes, feet, lower leg, and upper leg. Stretch and clench each muscle, then release until the muscle is free of stress and tension. Next move on to the muscles in your groin, abdomen, chest, shoulders, arms, and back. Finish by focusing on the face muscles, around your mouth, eyes, and forehead.

As you move from one muscle group to the next, you'll gradually become more relaxed, until your whole body is in a state of calmness. Your breathing will slow down and you'll begin to feel less sensation in your body, until you're ready to let go completely and fall asleep.

Use Relaxation Affirmations

Affirmations can be applied to almost any area of your life, including sleep. (Affirmations are discussed further in Chapter 6, "Tools for Motivation.") Sometimes when we have trouble sleeping we begin to have negative, self-fulfilling thoughts—"I'll never fall asleep" or "My mind is racing too much." We may start ruminating on such thoughts *before* we go to bed, so they become more and more difficult to overcome.

Instead of filling your head with negative thoughts, you can use affirmations to fill it with calm, relaxing thoughts. For example:

- "I am falling asleep."

- "My body and mind are becoming calm and relaxed."

- "All of my stress and anxiety are floating away."

These simple affirmations can prepare your body and mind to enter a state of sleep. Using such affirmations along with progressive muscle relaxation (described previously) can make that exercise even more effective.

Other Small Habits for Improving Sleep

Here are a few more ideas that have worked for some people. Try these out to see what works for you. Having healthy or unhealthy sleep habits can make or break the rest of your day.

Listen to calming sounds. Soothing sounds can help relax your mind so that you fall asleep more quickly. Back in my college days, I turned on a small fan when I struggled with sleeping. Nowadays, it's easy to find "sound generators" on your computer or cellphone that mimic waterfalls, ocean waves, rain, and other calming sounds to put on in the background when you want to fall asleep.

Create a wind-down routine. What you do *before* bedtime is important when it comes to your ability to fall asleep. It's helpful to create a tiny routine to help you unwind, de-stress, and prepare your body for sleep. Something as simple as dimming the lights, drinking a cup of green tea, brushing your teeth, and reading a chapter in a book can be an effective routine for winding down. Taking just a few minutes to sit down, look up at the stars, write in a journal, meditate/pray, or pet your dog can calm your mind and body before your head hits the pillow. Create a wind-down routine that works for you. The trick is to avoid doing anything too stimulating before bedtime.

Get comfortable. Though this may seem like simple common sense, it's a good reminder that you should optimize comfort as much as possible. Wear clothes that make you feel the most comfortable while sleeping, and make sure you have clean and comfortable bedding and pillows. Some people like to wear socks to stay warm, while others prefer to let their feet "breathe" throughout the night. Find the sleepwear that gives you the most personal comfort—and plan according to the temperature. If you know it's going to be a particularly cold night, put on an extra layer (or an extra blanket) so you won't wake up shivering in the middle of the night.

Place your alarm out of reach. One bad habit many people have when using an alarm is to hit the snooze button repeatedly and keep lying in bed, half asleep and half awake. One way to break this habit is to place your alarm where you have to get out of bed to turn it off. This simple trick will help you wake up faster and keep your sleep schedule more disciplined.

Pack a mental suitcase. One interesting tip I've learned is to pack a "mental suitcase" to take on an imaginary vacation. Go over in your mind what items you'll need: clothes, toothbrush, wallet, and so on. The monotony of this exercise can relax your mind and help you fall asleep.

Minimize internet and social media use. The internet and social media can become an addictive time warp. We open up YouTube or Facebook, and before we know it another two hours have passed. Try to avoid looking at your computer and/or phone as you approach the later hours of the night, when you want to get ready for sleep.

Can't fall asleep? Get up and do chores. If you've been lying in bed for more than 20 or 30 minutes and still feel energized and wide awake, it might be a good idea to get up and do some light chores, such as light cleaning or washing dishes. This can help burn off excess energy, and the monotony of the chore can calm your mind and make you feel sleepier.

Small Steps: Sleep

- Keep a regular sleep schedule
- Aim for 7 to 10 hours of sleep each night
- Set an alarm for going to bed as well as waking up
- Be physically active during the day so that you'll be tired at night
- Use your bedroom for sleeping, not for TV/computer use
- Make sure your pillows and sheets are clean and comfortable
- Brush your teeth and wash your face before you go to bed
- Dim the lights an hour before sleep time
- Stop using electronics 30 minutes before bedtime

- Have a light snack but no big meals before bed

- Read a book, meditate, or do something relaxing to wind down at the end of the day

- Take a calming bath to rest your body before you go to bed

- Open a window to let in fresh air while you sleep

- Close the blinds, turn off any lights, and make the room as dark as possible

- Play soothing sounds to help you fall asleep

- Visualize yourself in a relaxing place—at the beach, for instance, or staring at the stars

- Practice slow, deep breathing to calm your body and mind at bedtime

- Have a glass of water available by your bed

- Cuddle with a loved one, a pet, or even a stuffed animal

- If you can't sleep, get up and do something else for 15 minutes or so

Eating Habits

Eating is another one of those everyday habits that has a big effect on our physical health and mental well-being. A healthy diet can give you energy, motivation, and focus throughout the day, while an unhealthy diet can make you feel sluggish, irritable, and distracted. All of us should at least be mindful of what we are eating, because it has a real impact on how well we function throughout the day.

This book doesn't recommend any specific diet you should follow, and you should check with your doctor or a health professional before you make any major changes to your diet. But there are lots of things you can do to change your eating habits in small and healthy ways.

I think everyone already *knows*, deep down, how they should change their eating habits. Consuming lots of fast food, junk food, soda, beer, and sugary treats is obviously bad for you and your body. Most people don't need to read a special diet book to figure out what they should and shouldn't be eating. Instead, what most of us struggle with is actually following through and beginning to make different daily choices. It's about turning knowledge into action.

In this section, I suggest little ways you can begin changing your diet. The goal is to find *tiny changes* that can be sustained over time. It's common for dieters to try out a special program for a few months, make progress, and lose a lot of weight, but then slip back to their old eating pattern because they didn't plan for the long haul. Don't think of diet as a temporary thing you do to lose weight. Instead, think of it as changing your *lifestyle*. New habits need to become a part of who you are and how you see yourself in the future.

Pay Attention to How Your Body Responds

It's difficult, if not impossible, to recommend a specific diet that will work for everyone in the same way. Everyone's body is different, and everyone is going to respond to any diet in a different way. One of my core recommendations is to just *pay attention* to how your body responds to what you eat. If we listen more closely to what our body is saying after we consume a drink, meal, or snack, we can get a clearer idea of what effect it's having on us.

Find a diet that works with your stomach. If you find yourself feeling crummy and tired after a meal, it likely means you ate too much or in an unhealthy way. Listen to how your body is responding to what you ate. Ask yourself, "How do I feel? Do I feel more energized or less energized after consuming that?" This simple attitude can be one of the biggest shifts in how you approach food.

Slow Down

We tend to move fast these days in everything we do, and that includes eating.

Perhaps we are so preoccupied with work, family, and other responsibilities that eating a meal seems more like a necessary chore than anything else. So, we rush to finish as quickly as possible so we can move on to something we see as more productive. But eating is an activity that definitely deserves our attention.

For starters, eating more slowly and mindfully helps us to *enjoy* our food more. It gives us time to really experience flavors and textures and maximize the pleasure we get from eating tasty food. Even more importantly, eating slowly helps us to be more mindful of what and how much we are consuming.

It takes a little while before the brain registers that we're no longer hungry, so when you eat rapidly and mindlessly you are likely to consume a lot more than you need to fill you up. Fast eating can make you feel bloated and stuffed—and that's a sign of unhealthy eating. Simply slowing down can be a good way to consume less and give your body time to feel satisfied before you help yourself to seconds.

Serve Yourself Smaller Portions

Another simple trick for eating less is to give yourself smaller portions. The best way to do this is to use smaller plates and glasses so that you physically limit how much food and drink you can serve yourself at one time.

We tend to feel we need to finish our food and not waste any of it, so if you give yourself a huge plateful you're going to feel obligated to eat it all. You can easily avoid this by serving yourself less food *before* you begin eating. Then there's no incentive to eat more than you need.

This works both for full meals and for midday snacks. If you're watching a movie and want some potato chips (or whatever), that's fine—but instead of taking the whole bag, pour some chips into a smaller container. This will help you avoid the trap of constantly reaching into a bag of junk food that contains way more than you should consume in one sitting.

A big part of healthy eating, especially in a world where obesity and other problems associated with overeating are major concerns, is simply to eat less. And that begins with giving ourselves smaller portions.

Minimize Junk Food, Sugar, and Empty Calories

One of the biggest changes you can make to your diet is what you choose *not* to eat.

We intuitively know that certain drinks and foods aren't good for us, but one of the most difficult things is actually to avoid consuming them, or at least to minimize our consumption. I'm not against indulging in not-so-healthy pleasures now and then. An occasional candy bar isn't going to hurt you—the trick is to avoid letting it develop into a frequent, long-term habit.

I'm not going to lecture about how eating Skittles and French fries every day is bad for you. A quick Google search will show you numerous studies on the dangers of sugar and junk food. You already know that. But here are some ways to avoid consuming these things in excess:

Surround yourself with healthy foods. One of the easiest ways to avoid junk food is simply to stop buying it and having it available. If there aren't any unhealthy snacks in your home (or at school/work), then you won't have to worry about making that choice. Stock up on healthy options instead.

Drink more water and/or tea. Another small but fundamental change you can make is to drink more water and tea—especially if you substitute them for soda or sugary drinks that are just empty calories. Water is one of the most important things you should be consuming throughout the day; it keeps your body hydrated, clean, and feeling good. Tea and coffee can also be good substitutes for unhealthy snacks; they can curb your appetite, which is helpful if you're trying to eat less.

Pay attention to labels. Many of us consume food products without ever looking at the nutrition labels and asking ourselves, "What am I really putting inside my body?" When we finally do investigate, it can be a surprise to find out how many calories (or grams of sugar, fats, and sodium) are in a product—and what the intended serving size is. Develop the habit of checking the labels on food products to see what's in them before you consume them. Compare multiple products at the store before you buy one, and try to choose the healthier options.

Be around healthy people. One excellent way to change your eating habits is to spend your time with people who have healthy habits. Our daily relationships can have a major influence on our choices, so if we see a friend eating a bag of candy we're going to be much more motivated to get one for ourselves (monkey see, monkey do). This doesn't mean you need to ditch friends who have unhealthy habits, but it may be best to be around healthier people more frequently, especially at mealtimes.

Have a variety of choices. We eat junk food because it tastes good to us, but there are plenty of healthy foods and snacks that can be just as tasty. To keep your eating habits fun and interesting, experiment with different foods to find a variety of healthy choices that you enjoy. Variety can help to maximize the pleasure you get from eating, without requiring you to overconsume junk foods and sweets.

Consider a multivitamin. Ideally you should be getting adequate nutrients through your diet, but you may want to consider taking a

daily multivitamin just to be sure you're not deficient in any important vitamins or minerals. You should be able to find a comprehensive,
inexpensive multivitamin that has everything you'll need. It doesn't
hurt to take one a day so that you know your body is getting the fuel
it needs to function at its best.

The Benefits of Intermittent Fasting

Up to this point, most of my dietary suggestions have been focused on
making tiny changes, but here's a slightly bigger change to consider.

A recent phenomenon that's catching on in the health world is "intermittent fasting." The basic idea is to fast for short periods of time. A
typical recommendation is to fast for 16 hours each day and save all
of your eating for the other 8 hours. For example, you might choose
to eat between 10 a.m. and 6 p.m., then fast for the remainder of the
night and into the next morning. To help curb your appetite and stay
hydrated, you can drink water or green tea with a slice of lime during
the fasting period. But the main goal is to consume the bulk of your
calories within an 8-hour window.

Research has shown numerous benefits associated with intermittent
fasting, both physical (weight loss, reduced body fat, and better
heart functioning) and mental (increased focus, motivation, and self-
discipline). Intermittent fasting won't help everyone, but it may be
worth experimenting with, especially if one of your goals is to lose
weight. Starting is often the hardest part, so I recommend you try it
out on a weekend day when you don't have much to do, in case you
feel fatigued the first time you fast. Also, as I stated previously, you
should check with your doctor or a health professional before making
any drastic changes to your diet.

Like most of the ideas in this book, intermittent fasting isn't a require-
ment, but it's a change in habits that's worth trying if you want to
become a more disciplined eater.

Small Steps: Diet

- Drink water at every meal
- Eat a salad for your midday snack
- Limit fast food intake by 1x per week
- Substitute a sugary snack with yogurt or small fruit
- Cut your red meat consumption by 1x per week
- Don't add extra salt to your meals
- Plan and prepare your meals before the week starts
- Eat an early breakfast to get your metabolism going
- Cook your own meals instead of eating out
- Serve yourself smaller portions
- Eat slowly and mindfully—and notice when you are full
- Avoid snacking while you're distracted or watching TV
- Diet with a friend so that you can hold each other accountable
- Pay attention to how your body responds to different foods
- Avoid emotional eating—eat to nourish, not to cope
- Surround yourself with healthy snacks, at home and at work
- Surround yourself with people who have healthy habits
- Take a multivitamin daily
- Curb your appetite by drinking coffee or tea
- Try intermittent fasting on weekends or "off days"
- Avoid eating by yourself

- Make fruit/vegetable smoothies to help meet your nutritional needs

- Been good all day? Reward yourself with a dessert or "unhealthy snack"

Exercise

Like sleeping and eating, exercise is essential if we want to maximize our focus, energy, and motivation throughout the day. Everyone *knows* that being more physically active is good for us (and leads to a longer, healthier life), but many of us have trouble making regular exercise an integral part of our daily routine.

My focus is on small ways to begin building a more physically active lifestyle. When people start a new exercise routine, they often think they need to exercise for a specific amount of time every day or they've failed and there's no point in doing anything at all. They set a goal such as "go to the gym five times per week," even though they've never stepped foot in a gym. But trying to make huge changes overnight rarely works. Though you might be able to keep it up for a week or two, you're likely to get stressed and fatigued, and quickly go back to your old habits.

We fall into the trap of thinking of exercise as something we cram into our schedule two months before summer so we'll look good at the beach, not something that needs to become a daily part of who we are.

The "Everything Counts" Mindset

One of the most valuable pieces of advice when it comes to exercise is to take on the "everything counts" mindset. When you have this mindset, you permit yourself to do as much or as little exercise as possible—because *something is always better than nothing.*

Maybe you have only 15 minutes free today. Many people would think, "Oh well, I guess I don't have time to exercise." But those with an "everything counts" mindset will take that 15 minutes and do something with it—even if it's just going for a short walk or doing some jumping jacks. In fact, if you're someone who spends a lot of time sitting at home or at work, the simplest thing you can do is to stand up for a few minutes. Studies show that sitting for long periods of time is associated with various health risks. Just giving yourself permission to stand up and move around a bit can have an impact.

When you have an "everything counts" mindset, it's easy to find opportunities for exercise throughout your day.

Find Exercise that Fits Your Daily Life

Opportunities to be more physically active are all around us if we just pay attention.

Exercise doesn't have to be something that you schedule for a specific time of the day. It also doesn't have to be something that must be done in a specific place, like a gym or your basement. We can find ways to be physically active that fit naturally into our routines.

Could you ride your bike to work instead of driving? Could you take your dog on walks more frequently? Could you do more physical activities with your children, such as going to a park or playing sports? All of these fit into the "everything counts" mentality. You may not think of playing with your children as exercise, but it *can* be, as long as it gets you moving.

The exercise opportunities that you discover will depend on your own daily routine. What works for you may not work for someone else, and vice versa. Take a minute to think once again about your daily routine. What are some ways you can add more physical activity to your routine—even if it's just an extra 10 minutes?

Reframe Exercise from "Work" to "Fun"

We often think of exercise as "work" rather than something "fun." This can have a negative effect on our motivation when it comes to being more physically active.

An interesting study done by Cornell University's Food and Brand laboratory in 2014 discovered that when we reframe exercise as a "fun run" or a "scenic walk," we are less likely to snack on junk food afterwards. Because we don't see exercise as "work," we don't need to reward ourselves for doing it.

Naturally, when we enjoy something and it makes us feel good, we are more motivated to do it. We see the activity itself as its own reward. Maybe going to the gym by yourself or running on a treadmill seems like a tedious chore. But what about starting a softball team with friends? Or going on nature walks with your spouse, or joining a yoga class? Find physical activities you *enjoy* doing, and you'll find it much easier to be naturally active throughout your day. When you're doing something that brings you joy, you won't see it as a chore.

Think about the activities you enjoyed as a kid. That can be a good starting point for finding new activities that bring you joy. I really enjoyed baseball, so part of my new routine has been going to the batting cages and playing catch with my brother. The best part is that I don't see this activity as work at all. I'm driven to do it because I really enjoy it and it makes me *feel good*. Being fun doesn't mean it isn't exercise. Everything counts—even the fun stuff.

Applying These Principles

The principles in this section have really helped me put together my own health routine—one that fits with what I enjoy doing and is easy to work into my daily lifestyle. Here are some physical activities that I've been doing more frequently:

- Walking my dog

- Riding my bike to the store or library

- Going to the batting cages

- Throwing a baseball around

- Playing in the park with friends (and their kids)

- Doing pull-ups whenever I enter my bedroom

- Going on nature walks with friends

- Swimming in the pool or the ocean

- Playing billiards when people come over (better than sitting in front of the TV)

- Stretching before I take a shower

All of these work for me because they are both fun and convenient. While some are definitely more physically demanding than others, all of them give me a reason to get up and move around a little. The baseball activities stem from my enjoyment of sports as a boy. The nature walks and playing in the park are just good reasons to get out in the sunshine. Riding my bike instead of driving everywhere has been very rewarding—and I enjoy bike-riding a lot more than running!

It may not look like a rigorous workout routine, but for me these are all steps in the right direction. Everything counts. And most significantly? These habits are *sustainable* for me, because I enjoy them and they fit nicely into my daily routine. This is why the "everything counts" perspective is so important: it's not about working your butt off for a few months to lose weight, it's about building healthy habits that last a lifetime.

What are some small, fun, and easy exercises you could start adding to your own routine? What opportunities for physical activity are hidden throughout your day? Remember, it doesn't matter how small you start: everything counts.

Small Steps: Exercise

- Go for a one-mile walk before work

- Stretch to start your morning

- Do a rep of push-ups/jumping jacks/pull-ups between activities

- Avoid sitting too much—stand up frequently, even if it's only for a few minutes

- Take the stairs instead of an elevator

- Do physical activities you find fun (riding bike, swimming, tennis, etc.)

- Park farther away so you have to take a mini-walk to get where you want to go

- Do a rep of push-ups or sit-ups before you eat a snack

- Do a rep of pull-ups every time you enter your bedroom, office, etc.

- Join a sports league with friends

- Go to the gym with someone who will hold you accountable

- Hang out with fit people!

- Listen to music while you work out

- Whenever you can, walk or bike instead of driving

- Practice mind-body exercises, such as yoga or tai chi, to improve body awareness

- Do sports or other physical activities with your kids

- Play with your pets—take them on walks, bring them outside, play "wrestle"

- Spend time in nature, even if it's only at a local park

- Make love with your partner more often

==================

Wrapping Up the Basics

Sleeping, eating, and exercising are all incredibly important to get right if you want to maximize your health, happiness, and energy. Though a lot of the ideas in this chapter may seem like simple common sense, the real key is that they are all small and easy enough to begin in a single day. That makes them good starting points for self-change and self-improvement.

You should probably only focus on one tiny habit (or maybe two) at a time. Wait until that habit has become fully integrated into your daily routine and then you can move on to the next tiny change that you want to make.

Identify which of the three basic areas—sleep, diet, and exercise—you need to work on the most (think back to your "daily routine" exercise in Chapter 1), then focus on that. These areas all feed into each other, so don't be surprised if you notice a spillover effect. You may find that eating healthier food gives you more energy, so you feel more like exercising. And by exercising more, you may find that it's easier to fall asleep at night.

Every habit we take on influences the rest of our day in some small way.

When you topple over that first domino, it begins to knock the rest down as well. Find one small habit you can start working on *today* to build momentum and motivation. Then you can keep building off of that change, transforming it into something much bigger.

CHAPTER THREE

Habit Loops and Willpower

Almost every habit we have is driven by a formula that psychologists refer to as "habit loops." In this chapter you'll discover how we can use this framework to change old habits and build new ones.

The basic concept, according to Charles Duhigg in his popular book *The Power of Habit*, is that every habit can be broken down into three main parts: 1) Cue, 2) Routine, and 3) Reward. Here's a brief rundown on what each of these means:

- **Cue:** A stimulus from your environment that triggers your brain to perform the habit. (Example: A fun party influences you to want to drink alcohol.)

- **Routine:** The actual "habit" (a physical action) you follow whenever presented with the cue. (Example: Drinking alcohol.)

- **Reward:** The physical or mental benefit you get from following a particular habit. (Example: Drinking makes it easier to socialize.)

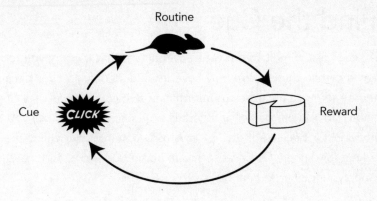

The Habit Loop

Often, we aren't even aware of these habit loops. We follow them without paying any conscious attention to what is leading us to the choices we make. But you'll find that every habit follows this "cue ⟶ routine ⟶ reward" pattern in one way or another. By better understanding your own particular habit loops, you can use this information to change any specific behavior.

Let's say that every day after dinner you sit on your couch to watch TV while eating a carton of ice cream. That's a dangerous habit—and probably the reason you've gained 25 pounds over the past few months. However, no matter how hard you try, you can't seem to break the habit.

What you need to do is identify your habit loop. What is the *routine* that you want to change? What are the *cues* triggering you to follow that routine? And what are the *rewards* you are getting as a result? By understanding the cycle of "cue ⟶ routine ⟶ reward," you can more easily modify your behavior.

Find the Cue

A "cue" is a stimulus from your environment that triggers you to follow a certain routine. We may have trouble identifying cues because there's so much unconscious information that can motivate any single habit. Do you eat dinner at a certain time each day because you are hungry? Or because the clock says 6:30 p.m., or your children start asking for dinner? Or because you're home from work, and that's just when your dinner routine begins?

Psychologists have identified different categories of cues that trigger our habit loops. If you are trying to find what cue is motivating a specific habit, consider these possible triggers:

- **Location**—Where are you when your habit loop is triggered?

- **Time**—What time of the day is it?

- **Mood**—What's your emotional state?

- **Thoughts**—What are you thinking?

- **People around you**—Who is around you when you act out this habit?

- **Preceding action**—What do you do immediately before the habit kicks in?

These are useful questions to ask yourself when you're trying to discover what starts a specific habit loop. Once you understand the cue that triggers your action, you can use that insight to begin to change the behavior. Say you discover that your habit of drinking is typically triggered by your location (party, bar, club) or by the people you are with (friends who love drinking). One way you can disrupt the habit loop is to avoid places or people that motivate you to drink.

Identifying the cue that triggers your behavior is a great first step to changing a specific habit, because you can either avoid exposing yourself to unhealthy cues or build new associations between those cues and different, healthier habits.

Try Out Different Rewards

It's also important to look at what reward each habit is giving you. Every habit has a perceived benefit, or we wouldn't be motivated to do it at all. Ask yourself, "What am I really getting out of this behavior? What are the perceived benefits?"

Let's go back to the example of eating ice cream while watching TV. By trying out different rewards, you can see what it is you get from that activity. Are you eating ice cream because you're hungry? Are you just bored, and it's a way to pass the time? Do you feel like you just need to "do something" while watching TV? Or is it what you do to socialize with family or roommates?

You may have to experiment with different rewards before you find out what it is you're really craving in that situation. Maybe you try eating a chicken salad instead of ice cream, but you still feel an urge for ice cream afterwards. This suggests that the reward you're getting from the ice cream isn't related to hunger. Next you might try socializing with family in a different way, such as playing a video game together. If your craving for ice cream goes away after this activity, your ice cream habit may be driven by the reward of socializing with family or friends.

This is one simple example, but you get the idea. People do things for many different reasons, but experimenting with different rewards can help us find what needs our brains actually want fulfilled. If we understand that, we can replace our old habit loops with new habit loops that still give us the rewards we actually want.

Make a Plan to Change Your Habit Loops

Once you identify the "cue ⟶ routine ⟶ reward" behind your habit loops, it becomes much easier to make a plan for changing them.

Compelling research by psychologists shows that having a plan to act a certain way at a certain time and place makes it far likelier that we will commit to new behaviors. Such plans are called "implementation intentions." The basic idea is to form an "if-then" plan to help instill new habits. Write down your plan and repeat it to yourself—"If situation X arises, I will perform response Y." X refers to the cue you get from your environment; Y is the new routine you want to follow instead of your former habit.

For example, when it comes to eating ice cream while watching TV, your new plan might be, "If I'm watching TV, then I'll fix myself a healthy salad or have some yogurt." By creating a plan, writing it down, and repeating it to yourself, you'll be more likely to carry out the new behavior when you find yourself in that situation again. The next time you get ready to watch TV, you're already thinking to yourself, "I'll prepare a healthy snack."

You might make mistakes along the way. Don't be too hard on yourself when trying to change habits, especially really sticky ones. Maybe some days you'll miss your cue and forget your new plan. Maybe other days you'll find it easier just to resort to your old habit. It's reasonable to expect that it's going to take some practice before your new habit loop becomes automatic.

As Charles Duhigg writes in his book *The Power of Habit*: "Habits aren't destiny—they can be ignored, changed, or replaced. But it's also true that once the loop is established and a habit emerges, your brain stops fully participating in decision-making. So, unless you deliberately fight a habit—unless you find new cues and rewards—the old pattern will unfold automatically."

Simply understanding how habit loops work makes this process easier. There will always be some self-discipline and patience needed to get the results you want. Don't be surprised if you stumble a bit. Remember that you're trying to rewire your brain—and that takes time.

Habit Stacking: Combining New and Old Habits

When it comes to our daily routine, one habit loop often feeds directly into another habit loop.

If you remember, one of the main cues that can trigger a habit is the immediately preceding action. This means that we sometimes perform a habit simply because it tends to follow another habit in our daily routine. Maybe after you brush your teeth in the morning you usually go take a shower. By doing these habits back-to-back for a long period of time, they become inherently linked together— almost as if they are a single habit loop.

Interestingly, a new concept known as "habit stacking" follows this same principle, and it's an excellent way to build new habits into your routine. The idea is to link a new habit that you want to establish with another habit that's already part of your routine.

So if you want to build a new habit, find an already consistent habit with which to pair it. Set up a plan similar to "implementation intentions," discussed above, but frame it as "After I do X, I will do Y" or "Before I do X, I will do Y." Here are a few examples of habit stacking:

- Before I take a shower, I will do 10 push-ups.

- After I exercise, I will meditate for 10 minutes.

- Before I eat a meal, I will take a minute to reflect on something I'm grateful for.

- After I drink my cup of coffee, I will answer emails.

- Before I go to bed, I will write for 10 minutes in my journal.

Each of these examples combines an old habit with a new habit. That's the key. These are just a few examples, but the possibilities are endless. Once you've created a strong association between the old habit and the new one, you'll begin to do them together naturally and automatically.

Willpower

The ability to change our habits is an important part of cultivating a healthy and happy life, but there are many factors to consider when trying to change yourself. Identifying your habit loops is a good start, but that won't always be enough. Willpower plays a key role in all habit change.

"Willpower" is the self-discipline to do something even when you don't *feel* like doing it. For example, those who have strong willpower in a given situation will be able to resist that slice of cake or push themselves to go to the gym, while someone with less willpower may find these behaviors more difficult if they aren't part of a regular routine.

Recently there has been a good amount of research on how we can maximize our willpower when trying to change habits. The popular book *Willpower: Rediscovering the Greatest Human Strength* by psychologist Roy F. Baumeister gives an excellent breakdown of this research and tells us how we can apply it to our daily lives.

Here are the important findings:

Willpower is a limited resource that needs to be used wisely. When researchers had participants resist eating a cookie, afterwards the participants performed worse on a difficult puzzle. When we exercise our willpower for one task, it turns out, we have less willpower to dedicate to another task. Therefore, it's best to focus on changing just one major habit at a time. If you spread yourself thin by trying to change too much at once, it's likely that you will become tired and give up on your goals sooner.

Willpower can be strengthened, like a muscle. Although it's true that our willpower is limited, we can build our long-term capacity by actively exercising our willpower. Practice by changing small habits first—like replacing soda with water or going for a walk every morning. You can move on to bigger habits once your willpower and motivation have been strengthened. It's like exercising any other muscle. You can't expect to bench-press 200 pounds the first time you go to the gym, but if you work at it, then one day you might be able to do it. Our willpower works the same way. We have to exercise it to build up its strength and cultivate self-discipline.

Believing you have more willpower makes you push yourself harder. A study published in the scientific journal *Proceedings of the National Academy of the Sciences* in 2013 found that students could fight off taking a study break simply by having the mindset that they could go longer. When motivating ourselves to change habits, it's important to remember that our attitude and beliefs play a crucial role. If you believe that you can achieve something, you're more likely to push yourself to go that extra mile. But when you believe your willpower is weak, you're likely to settle for less and give up, because you don't feel you have it in you to succeed. So even though our willpower might technically be limited, it's still helpful to cultivate the mindset that you can draw on unlimited energy—especially when you're trying to run that last mile or resist that unhealthy snack late at night.

Practice taking a step back. One of the best ways to disconnect from our routines and change our behavior is to practice a short "STOP meditation." This is when we step back from what we are doing in the moment and reflect on our current mindset. Set an alert on your phone (or computer) and use it as a reminder to step back and ask yourself, "What am I doing? What am I thinking? What am I feeling? What am I trying to accomplish?" Then you can go back to what you were doing with a fresh outlook. Willpower requires focus and awareness; if you go about your day unconsciously, without ever second-guessing yourself, then you aren't exercising much of your willpower and potential. Sometimes we need to step back before we can choose a new direction.

Once you build one habit, you can concentrate your willpower on another. Habits are characterized by being routine and automatic. When you first learned how to tie your shoes, it may have taken a lot of effort and concentration. But now that you've done it so many times, it's second-nature to you—and therefore takes practically no willpower or energy. In the same way, once we successfully build a new habit, we no longer need as much willpower to carry it out. Instead, we can begin focusing that willpower on new behaviors. One of the big lessons behind the psychology of willpower is that we should focus on just one major life change at a time.

Creating Boundaries between You and Your Bad Habits

Though willpower is an important aspect of changing yourself for the better, you only have a certain amount of willpower to use in the course of your day. Once it runs dry, you need to let yourself relax and reboot before your willpower "reservoir" builds up again. In one study published in *Psychological Science* in 2013, it was found that people tend to be more ethical in the morning and less ethical by the afternoon. Our ability to resist temptation diminishes throughout the day—and this applies not only to unethical behavior, but to any habit we are trying to resist.

If you can't always rely on sheer willpower, what can you do? One tool you can use is to create *boundaries* between you and your unwanted habits. By doing this, you can stop a habit loop before it gets started. The goal is to make it increasingly difficult (or impossible) to give in to the bad habit, even if you really, really want to.

Obviously, it's harder to eat junk food if you don't keep your home and office stocked with candy, chips, and ice cream. In the same way, it's harder to fall back into a drug habit if you cut off your contacts with friends and dealers who can provide you with said substance.

Create situations in which it's nearly impossible to carry out your bad habit. The more boundaries, the more difficult, the better. At first it may hurt not to get what you want, but gradually you'll learn other ways to live your life and fulfill your needs. Boundaries can force you to adapt to new situations in a positive way.

This is why people who've just gotten out of a bad relationship block their ex on Facebook, delete the ex's number from their phone, or stop hanging out with friends from their old social circle. We can't always trust ourselves to change, even when we know we should. We're imperfect. Situational factors can outweigh the best of intentions, so it's helpful to find ways to avoid putting ourselves in certain situations *before* they become a problem.

Another example of setting up boundaries to alter habits is the use of email and website blockers to avoid procrastination at work. How often do you find yourself checking your email or Facebook or Twitter? Imagine how helpful it would be if you could temporarily make these time-suckers off limits. If you do an internet search for "block site plugins," you can find something that will work with your browser to help you avoid wasting time on unproductive websites.

Be creative. As long as you can identify the triggers behind your undesirable habits, you can find ways to avoid those triggers. That way you'll be able to circumvent your negative patterns altogether.

Small Steps: Cleaning

- Make your bed every morning

- Sell, donate, or throw out any possessions you don't need anymore

- Don't leave a room without cleaning up after yourself

- Wash your dishes as soon as you finish eating

- Throw dirty clothes directly into the laundry bin

- Split cleaning duties if you live with others

- Listen to music to make cleaning more fun

- Open your windows to let in fresh air

- Use flowers and plants to fill your home with nice scents

- To let go of a sentimental object, take a picture of it and save it

- Always clean up after yourself when you're a guest in someone else's home

- Remove your shoes indoors

- Save important papers (tax documents, contracts, receipts) in a filing cabinet

- Do laundry once per week—don't let it pile up

- Launder your bed sheets weekly

- Put things away as soon as you finish using them

- Don't let any mess build up over time

- Dedicate a chunk of time each week to cleaning

- Once a year, devote a day to a "tidying marathon"

CHAPTER FOUR

Morning Ritual: Start Every Day on the Right Note

If your daily routine is a symphony, then your morning is the first note of the day—and it's important that it be the right one.

Your morning can make or break your entire day. If you start out feeling stressed and tired, you're going to have a difficult time getting through the rest of your daily routine and making the most out of your waking hours. In this chapter, I want to focus on developing a morning ritual that works for you, energizes you, and gives you positive momentum as you enter your day.

Mornings are a good time of the day to focus on, because we may have a little extra time to ourselves then to work on self-improvement and change our overall attitude before beginning the day. But before I offer tips on developing your own morning ritual, I want to draw a distinction between "routines" and "rituals."

Routines vs. Rituals

Throughout this book I use the word "routine" to describe a series of habits, because that's the way we commonly think of the term. However, I often use the words "ritual" and "routine" interchangeably, and sometimes I prefer "ritual" because I find it more empowering and impactful. That's why in this chapter I refer to a "morning ritual" rather than a "morning routine."

The big difference between a ritual and a routine is not necessarily the action, but the attitude behind the action. To many, a routine is getting up every morning, eating breakfast, brushing teeth, taking a shower, getting dressed, and going to work. It is not a meaningful part of our day, but it needs to get done and so we do it. It's viewed as a chore.

Rituals, on the other hand, are seen as more meaningful practices. Often there is symbolism involved, and a sense of purpose. A big part of a ritual is one's subjective experience of the activity.

Here are the principal differences I see between routines and rituals.

ROUTINES	RITUALS
Minimal engagement	Full engagement
Tedious and meaningless	Symbolic and meaningful
Externally motivated	Internally motivated
Life as a duty	Life as a celebration
Dull awareness	Bright awareness
Disconnected series of events	Tells a story
Little sense of belonging	Sense of belonging
Focus only on completion of tasks	Focus on performance of tasks

Though we often associate rituals with religion or spirituality (and that can certainly be a component of your mornings), I believe we can transform any routine into a ritual, given the right attitude. Instead of viewing every daily activity as something that "just needs to get done," you can begin to appreciate that those regular behaviors serve a positive function in your life.

Even brushing your teeth can be seen as a meaningful activity that symbolizes important things—taking caring of your body, loving yourself, and presenting your best self. The more meaning you find in your daily activities, the more motivated you become to do them. Try to step back and see the bigger picture behind your daily activities, and how they serve and improve your life as a whole. This can add meaning and positivity to everything you do.

Your Own Morning Ritual

Now let's get to work creating a morning ritual that works for you. A good starting point is to revisit the daily routine exercise from Chapter 1 and examine how you start most of your mornings now. Then you can decide what tiny adjustments you might like to make.

Ask yourself this: "What do I really need in the morning to get my day started on the right note?" Your morning needs may include preparing yourself for the day (eating, showering, getting dressed, brushing teeth), enjoying a little peace and relaxation (drinking tea and watching the news or listening to music), getting in some physical activity (going for a walk or going to the gym), doing motivation exercises (affirmations, visualizations), or a combination of these things.

First, let me share my own morning ritual and how each activity serves my overall day:

- **Wake up!** Obviously, this is the first step to every morning.

- **Make my bed.** It's good to complete a small task to start the day with a sense of accomplishment (and it just makes things look nice).

- **Walk my dog.** A necessity for me, but it feels nice to step outside, get some fresh air, and move around a little to wake up my body and mind. And spending time with the pup usually puts me in a good mood.

- **Drink coffee and listen to music.** Nice "alone time" to relax, spend time with my thoughts, and enjoy a few moments of peace before I start my day. (This part of my "ritual" usually lasts from 15 to 30 minutes, depending on how much time I have.)

- **Mindful stretching.** I usually spend 10 minutes doing some stretching to wake up my body and get the blood flowing. Nothing intense, just giving my body a quick "Hi, wake up!"

- **Push-ups/pull-ups/sit-ups.** After I'm done stretching, I'll push my body a little further by doing a few reps of push-ups, pull-ups, and sit-ups. This is a great mini-workout for me in the morning, especially if I won't have other opportunities throughout the day to be physically active.

- **Eat breakfast.** Many people skip breakfast, but it's an important meal for me to get my body in full gear. I usually prepare something really quick (eggs, fruit, etc.) and may have the news on in the background to get a quick idea of what's going on in the world.

- **Shower/brush teeth.** Taking care of personal hygiene is typical morning stuff. I usually enjoy this as a time to reflect on what I want to do that day, as well as give myself a bit of a pep talk and feed myself positive thoughts.

- **Affirmations/pep talk.** This is just a quick "positive talk" inside my head, simple things like "You are empowered to do your best today" and "You will stay focused on what needs to be done in the moment." I treat it as a motivational speech that a coach would give to me before a big game. (I often do this in the shower or right after.)

- **Drink a glass of water and take vitamins.** A good way to make sure my body is replenished and rejuvenated before I start my day.

- **Get to work.** This is when my morning ritual ends and my productive day officially begins.

This is a brief summary of my own morning ritual, which usually takes no more than 60 to 90 minutes. There's nothing fancy or unique about my ritual, but it works for me and gets me in the right mental state to start my day. Your morning ritual may look quite different. A lot depends on your own personality and what works best for you, as well as how much time you have to yourself and what other responsibilities you have.

Some people prefer to read the newspaper, watch a morning show on TV, or do some cleaning. Some call their mom/dad, engage in yoga/meditation/prayer, or wake up an hour early to go to the gym. I recommend a mix of physical activity and mental activity so that you get both body and mind awake and ready to go. However, the specific activities don't really matter as long as you are starting your morning on a positive note that makes you feel ready to conquer your day.

Your mornings will always vary a bit from day to day, especially if unexpected responsibilities come up. But the main goal is to create a rough version of your "ideal" routine.

exercise
Creating Your Morning Ritual

STEP **1.** Revisit your "Daily Routine" exercise from Chapter 1, focusing specifically on your morning habits.

STEP **2.** Reflect on your current morning ritual. Ask yourself:

- "Is my current morning ritual enough to get me energized and ready to start my day?"
- "Is my current morning ritual stimulating both my body and mind?"
- "How much time do I need to prepare for my day? Am I waking up at a good time?"

STEP **3.** Now take a piece of paper and pen (or open up a new text document on your computer) and write the heading "Morning Ritual" on your document.

STEP **4.** Make a step-by-step list of your ideal morning ritual, starting with "Wake Up." You can look at my ritual for ideas, but keep in mind that you want to create something that works for *you*.

- If your mornings are lacking physical stimulation, consider adding physical activities such as yoga, stretching, walking, or other exercise.
- If your mornings are lacking mental stimulation, consider adding reading, meditation, prayer, affirmations, or a "pep talk."
- Include all basic habits related to health and hygiene, such as eating, showering, brushing your teeth, flossing, getting dressed, taking your medication/vitamins.
- Consider whether you can stack certain habits together, such as doing affirmations while showering.

STEP **5.** Once you've completed your list, think about how each habit in your morning ritual serves your life. Save the document in your self-improvement folder.

You've completed the exercise. Great job!

Morning rituals can last anywhere from 15 minutes to several hours, depending on the needs of the individual. They don't have to be complicated, but you should pay attention to them, because they can influence the tone for the rest of your day. Be willing to experiment and try out new things. Find a ritual that works for you and your particular personality, needs, wants, and responsibilities.

CHAPTER FIVE

The Power of Nudges

In psychology, a "nudge" is any small change in our environment that can influence our behavior and decision-making. Nudges are of growing interest in the study of how to change people's behaviors in small and subtle ways (especially without the use of government mandates or economic incentives). Many organizations—including governments, businesses, schools, and nonprofits—are beginning to harness the power of nudges to influence people's choices.

As an illustration, one example of using a nudge is when a school cafeteria places healthy food at eye level and less healthy foods in harder-to-see places. This small change in the environment actually influences students to choose the healthier foods, simply because they are more accessible.

The book *The Last Mile: Creating Social and Economic Value from Behavioral Insights* by behavioral scientist Dilip Soman is a fantastic review of the research done on nudges thus far. It lays the foundation for understanding how individuals and organizations can begin using the power of nudges to influence choices in positive ways.

Some nudges are created by businesses to influence consumers, or by governments to influence citizens. Individuals can use nudges on themselves to change their own behavior. This chapter describes both "mindless nudges" (small changes that can *unconsciously* influence our choices) and "mindful nudges" (small changes that can *consciously* influence our choices).

Whereas none of these nudges are *necessary* for changing your habits, they can be helpful tools and aids to make habit change easier—especially if you combine them with your broader knowledge about how habit loops work. My recommendation is to focus on one major habit you are trying to change and then identify just one nudge that you could begin applying to make that change just a bit easier.

Remember—start small, think gradually, and you will begin to make big changes over time.

Mindless Nudges

Mindless nudges are ways of influencing behavior that occur outside of our conscious awareness. These are subtle ways of presenting a choice that can significantly influence our attitudes and decisions. By becoming more conscious of these nudges—and taking the time to change them—we can better set ourselves up for happiness, health, and success in almost any area of our lives.

Default Choice. One of the most common nudges is to make a desired behavior the "default" option. When people use a new product, service, or website, they are much more likely to keep the default settings than to change them. It's easier to stay with the status quo. This is a powerful nudge that many social media sites use to gather consumer data. When you sign up for many websites, you automatically agree to let your information be shared. Similarly, it's been shown that organ donations increase if individuals are presented with this choice as a default option when they get their driver's license.

Applying to your daily life: Change the default settings on your technology to what best serves you and your life goals. For example, change your internet homepage from something unproductive

(Twitter/Facebook) to something more productive. Pay attention to the default settings on your computer, phone, and other devices. Are they serving your goals or hurting them?

Framing. Another common nudge is to present a situation from a different perspective, called "framing." For example, research has shown that people are more motivated to make a decision if it is framed in terms of minimizing potential losses rather than maximizing potential gains. This is known in psychology as "loss aversion." So, to change behavior, presenting a situation in terms of what someone will *lose* or miss out on may be better than focusing on what they will *gain*.

Applying to your daily life: Try to frame your habits and goals in ways that motivate and inspire you. Instead of deciding to go to the gym just to be healthy, frame it as a bigger goal: "I want to be there for my family and friends as long as possible." Seeing your goal from the perspective of helping not just yourself but other people as well can be a powerful frame. Try writing out multiple frames for your current life goals and then choose what most resonates with you.

Environment. Anything in our environment can be a potential influence on our thoughts and behaviors. Studies have given us a wide range of examples, including how a picture of eyes on a wall can influence people to act more ethically and donate more generously to a charity. (The feeling of being watched can exert a powerful influence on human behavior.) Another study showed that a man holding a guitar was seen as being more attractive than a man who wasn't. These little environmental nudges can influence our decision-making.

Applying to your daily life: Pay attention to your surroundings, especially the places where you spend a lot of time (such as your bedroom, work office, car). Are these environments keeping you motivated and serving your goals? Choose furniture and decor that will fill your mind with good feelings throughout the day, without your even being conscious of it. If you're trying to improve your health, find motivating posters about exercise and eating right. Remember—your mind is picking up these environmental signals, so the atmosphere around you can make a big difference in your overall attitude.

Social Influence. A big motivator of our choices is social influence. When we see other people behaving a certain way, we tend to mimic their decisions. This is known as the "bandwagon effect." On an unconscious level we think, "Well, if lots of other people are making this choice, then it must be a good choice and I'll make it, too." In one case study, researchers made phone calls to increase voter participation. One script emphasized that voter turnout was expected to be low, while the other script said that turnout was expected to be high. It turned out that when voters were told that participation was expected to be high, they were far more likely to participate themselves.

Applying to your daily life: The people you surround yourself with can have a big impact on your own life choices. We really do follow the old cliché, "monkey see, monkey do." If you only hang out with people who eat lots of junk food and never exercise, you'll be way more likely to do the same. But if you hang out with people who are physically active and eat in a healthy way, it's going to be easier for you to do so, too. Research shows that our social networks often shape who we are and who we become. After all, we are social creatures who want to fit in with other people and be accepted by the group. Associating with successful, happy, and healthy people motivates you to adopt habits that will make you successful, happy, and healthy, too.

Priming. When exposure to one stimulus in our environment influences how we respond to a succeeding stimulus, that's called "priming." This happens without our being conscious of it. For example, individuals presented with the word "doctor" are primed to respond more quickly to the next word if it is "nurse" than if it is "bread," because there's a strong association between "doctor" and "nurse." The basic idea is that the first stimulus we receive in a situation can put us into the mindset to act a certain way toward the next stimulus.

Applying to your daily life: This is similar to the previous advice about paying attention to your environment, but in this case, you want to focus on the initial stimulus you expose yourself to before you begin an activity. For example, a poster of an athlete will prime you to push yourself harder at the gym than will a poster of someone reading a book. Choose a specific behavior you want to improve and find ways to prime your brain to perform the desired new habit. Our brains are highly susceptible to cues from the environment. Be mindful of that as you go about your day and prepare for your various activities.

Mindful Nudges

Mindful nudges are ways of changing human behavior that usually require conscious awareness *in the moment*. Many of us make decisions without really thinking or second-guessing ourselves. Mindful nudges require us to step back and reevaluate exactly what type of choice we want to make *before* we make a final decision.

Boundaries. The more steps it takes to make a choice, the harder it is to commit to that choice. Applying this simple principle can be an effective way to curb bad habits. By creating extra boundaries between ourselves and our bad choices, we make it increasingly difficult to continue making those choices. Putting a lock on the cabinet where you keep junk food, for example, means that you have to take that extra step of unlocking your cabinet before you indulge. This small boundary gives you a little more time to evaluate your decision before you act on it. In the same way, having junk food readily available (such as a jar of M&M's on your desk) makes unhealthy eating more likely, because the fewer the boundaries that stand in your way, the easier that decision is. Boundaries can help you avoid bad habits and develop better ones.

Applying to your daily life: Choose something you want to do less of or cut out completely and find ways to create multiple boundaries between you and that habit. The more boundaries you can come up with the better, because that will make you more likely to choose a better habit instead.

Earmarking. Earmarking is a useful way to become more conscious of how we spend our money and time. A basic example is separating earnings into different categories: Groceries, Rent, College, Leisure, Savings, and so on. When we assign money to a particular use, our minds are more committed to using the money that designated way. In one study it was found that when individuals received pay in two envelopes and one was marked "Savings," they were much more likely to save money than were those who received all their pay in a single unmarked envelope. By separating our money into budget categories, we can curb excessive consumption and save appropriately. You can apply this same concept to how you spend your time, earmarking hours for Work, Family, or Hobbies so that your mind is committed to certain activities at certain times.

Applying to your daily life: If you have money or time-management problems, earmarking is definitely a good commonsense approach to divvying up your resources and holding yourself accountable. Take the time to write out your earmarks and save them as a reminder. One popular use of earmarking is to designate a percentage of your monthly earnings to savings so that you don't mindlessly consume your entire paycheck.

Partitioning. Partitioning is a little like earmarking, but it's focused on dividing items of consumption into smaller parts—especially when it comes to eating and drinking. Using smaller plates and glasses for dinner often influences people to choose smaller portions and eat less overall. Similarly, people will eat less of a snack if they portion it out into smaller bags. Think about it: Eating one big bag of popcorn is only one decision, and once you commit to it you'll be tempted to finish the whole thing. Psychologically, our minds want to finish what we start. But eating three small bags of popcorn is three separate decisions, so it's easier to cut yourself off after just one bag. Research shows that increasing the number of decision points encourages more mindful consumption of food and drink, or even things like TV and the Web. You could limit TV consumption, for instance, by setting your TV to ask every 45 minutes or so whether you want to turn it off.

Applying to your daily life: Identify one thing that you tend to over-consume, like a particular food or drink, then find ways to partition that into smaller units. Take that big bag of chips and separate it into a dozen smaller bags. By doing this, you are committing yourself to smaller portions at a time, so you'll have to make a whole new decision if you want seconds or thirds.

Alerts. Setting up an alert on your watch, phone, tablet, or computer can be a powerful nudge to make us conscious of our daily choices. If you have trouble focusing at work, you may want to set your computer to alert you every two or three hours. This can serve as a reminder that you need to complete a certain project (or simply get back to work) and should probably get off of Facebook, Twitter, or whatever else is distracting you. This is one small way to inject greater consciousness into your daily activities. Whenever an alert goes off, you are forced to evaluate what you are doing in the present moment and make a decision about continuing that or starting something else.

Applying to your daily life: Use alerts as a general "injection of consciousness" to help you step back and evaluate what you are doing at the moment (especially during the times of the day when you typically get distracted). Or use them as a reminder to follow through on a specific habit that you are trying to build—setting an alert an hour before you should go to the gym, for example, or start your homework. If you get three alerts within an hour reminding you that you're supposed to be exercising, you're going to be way more motivated to fulfill that duty than if you simply try to shove it out of your mind. Use alerts to stay on track and hold yourself accountable.

Virtual Progress. To stay committed to our goals, it helps if we can see that we are making progress toward reaching those goals. Otherwise, we're likely to ditch the decision and walk away. When people are waiting on the phone to speak to customer service or standing in line at the DMV, they want to know that their commitment isn't in vain. By creating "progress points"—such as signposts or estimated times—these places let customers see that progress is being made. This feeling of progress is also why many people become addicted to mobile apps and games. Receiving immediate feedback and reaching checkpoints can shoot dopamine into our brains and motivate us to keep playing.

Applying to your daily life: An emerging concept in self-improvement is known as "gamification." This is the process of trying to make your life and goals more like a video game, in which you earn points to get to the "next level." You might assign points to specific habits that you are trying to build, then at the end of the day tally up the points you've earned. After you get to a certain number of points or reach a particular milestone, you can give yourself a reward (maybe a "treat yourself" day, or something nice that you buy for yourself). A lot of mobile apps nowadays also use gamification to help with motivation and habit-building. One popular example is Fitbit, for tracking health and fitness data. Another one I hear a lot about is Habitica, which applies RPG (role-playing game) elements to various habits and goals. It's actually fun and motivating to think of yourself as the hero of your own video game. Try doing an internet search for "Gamification Habit Apps" to find a range of mobile apps. The point is to find or create a system that lets you measure your progress so that you can feel a sense of accomplishment, see evidence that you're moving forward, and stay motivated.

Small Steps: Money

- Save at least 10 percent of every paycheck
- Budget for all your expenses every month
- Shop at thrift stores and garage sales

- Make food at home instead of eating out
- Don't buy stuff just to signal affluence or status
- Find a job that offers upward mobility
- Start a side project to make some extra income
- Be mindful of credit card use, and don't let debt build up
- Find cheap or free things to do on the weekends
- Have a garage sale to sell things you don't need
- Keep the future in mind—don't just consume for the present
- Learn how to fix your own furniture and appliances
- Use hand-me-downs from family and friends
- Take good care of your belongings so they'll last longer
- Learn to cut your own hair
- Focus on buying experiences, not stuff
- Buy a car that's reliable and economical
- Store and reuse leftover food rather than throwing it out
- Take advantage of discounts or sales for things you're already planning to buy
- Always carry some extra money hidden away in your wallet
- Don't gamble money you're not willing to lose
- Keep back-up money somewhere in your house to use for emergencies
- Invest your savings in safe ways
- Remember money is just a tool, it's up to you how you use it

CHAPTER SIX

Tools for Motivation

You now have a good understanding of how habits work and what strategies you can use to begin changing them. What you've learned can be hugely effective, but it always helps to have extra tools at your disposal to keep you energized, feeling good, and putting your best foot forward. This chapter offers a variety of motivational tools. Many of these are simple, easy, and even fun to work into your daily routine—and they can play a big role in boosting your positive emotions.

Different tools work better in different situations, depending on your mood and what you're trying to accomplish. For now, focus on *one* of the tools described in this chapter and find a way to apply it to your everyday life.

Affirmations and Quotes

In self-improvement terminology, an affirmation is simply a positive statement that we repeat back to ourselves to influence our thoughts, feelings, and overall mindset.

Our minds don't always think in a positive direction, so it helps to write out supportive thoughts and then carve out a little time in the day to recite them back to ourselves, either out loud or in our heads. By actively practicing this form of constructive thinking, we can create new pathways in our brains that make these thoughts come to us naturally and spontaneously.

There's nothing magical about affirmations—they are simply words you can use to help change your outlook. It's similar to reading an inspiring quote from your favorite athlete, scientist, philosopher, teacher, or musician. Look for words that inspire you. Something as simple as "I will do my absolute best today" can give you extra motivation as you start your day.

Here are just a few affirmations from my personal collection. You'll likely recognize a couple of these sayings, but this should give you an idea of the various ways you can use them.

- *"Every day, in every way, I'm getting better and better."* This classic affirmation was created in 1920 by French psychologist Émile Coué, who first popularized the idea of positive self-talk.

- *"No pain, no gain."* A common affirmation for those trying to push themselves through temporary pain or stress in order to achieve a goal, this one is especially appropriate when it comes to exercise or fitness. We may have to experience some physical strain before we can build muscles or lose weight.

- *"This too shall pass."* A popular mantra for those going through difficult times, this thought has definitely saved me when I've felt like I was stuck in a hopeless situation or in a really bad mood.

- *"Small changes on a daily basis lead to big changes over time."* This is a personal affirmation that I'm constantly repeating to myself—and it fits perfectly with the theme of this book.

- *"Each day is a new opportunity to put my best foot forward."* Another personal affirmation that I use all the time, these words help me see each day as a clean slate with which I can do whatever I want.

- *"Just do it."* You'll recognize this slogan from Nike commercials. It is used by many as motivation to take action and not overthink things—a common problem for those of us seeking to improve ourselves.

As you can see, an affirmation can come from anywhere. It can be a quote from someone famous, a line from a movie or book, a business slogan, a positive statement that you've created on your own, or just something someone once said that really affected you. Words that inspire one person won't necessarily inspire another, so don't just copy random affirmations off the internet. Search for ones that truly speak to you personally.

Making the Most of Your Affirmations

Affirmations can be an effective tool that is worth trying out and integrating into your day—and they don't take much time or effort to practice. They aren't *necessary* by any means, but they can be a fun and easy way to boost your motivation. Here are some ideas for using them.

Create your own collection. Put together a personal collection of "Positive Affirmations and Quotes" and save them on your computer or in the self-improvement folder you've created. Start by writing out three to five affirmations that feel meaningful to you, and then keep adding from there. My current collection includes more than 300 affirmations collected over the years. This has proven to be a fantastic resource when I need a shot of motivation and positivity.

Recite them during your morning ritual. The most common way to use affirmations is to recite them aloud or internally for 5 to 10 minutes. Simply choose three affirmations that resonate with you on a given day, then boldly recite each one several times—with purpose, meaning, and enthusiasm. This is a habit that's really simple to add to your morning ritual. You can easily practice your affirmations while you are taking a shower, brushing your teeth, or driving to work.

Post them around your home or office. Choose a few affirmations that you especially like, write them on sticky notes or index cards, and post them where you'll see them throughout the day—on a mirror or the fridge, above your bed, by your computer screen, in your car, and so on. Think of these as "positivity reminders."

Create positive passwords. One neat trick is to create passwords that are small affirmations. That way, every time you sign on to your computer, email, or social media, you'll be typing out a positive message to yourself. You might choose passwords like "IGrowEveryDay!" or "ILiveInThePresent!" or "TheBestVersionOfMe." Be creative, but make sure you're creating strong passwords that can't be hacked easily.

Experiment with different words. Remember, the key is to recite words and phrases that have a strong emotional impact for you. Experiment by changing some of the words in familiar affirmations to see if you can make them more powerful for you. Try using bold and exaggerated language to strengthen the message. Have fun with this! You can even throw in a curse word if you really want to.

List-Making

Writing is a useful way to keep our minds focused, organized, and thinking clearly. It's easy to get "stuck in our heads" when we're thinking to ourselves. ("Oh...I need to do this, this, and this tomorrow.") Writing gives us a way to turn fuzzy and abstract thoughts into something more concrete. (1. Take out the trash. 2. Pick up Tommy from school. 3. Go to doctor's appointment.)

List-making, in particular, is a simple yet effective way to keep our minds focused. You can find insightful examples of this in Atul Gawande's book *The Checklist Manifesto: How to Get Things Right*. Gawande describes how the simplicity of a checklist has revolutionized a wide range of fields, from public health to aviation, cooking to architecture.

List-making helps keep us from overlooking the basics, taking things for granted, or losing track of what's important. Our minds can become distracted by the wrong things, so a short list is one way to keep them looking in the right direction, no matter what we are trying to achieve. Lists can also remind us of things that motivate, inspire, and give us energy and passion.

Lists for Motivation and Inspiration

There are many ways we can use lists to help guide our lives and keep us focused. I recommend that you make at least one of the following lists and save it in your self-improvement folder. You can always go back and change or add to your lists in the future. Nothing you write is irreversible—these are just *tools* to get your mind thinking in the right direction.

The more you build off of these lists, the more powerful they will become. Imagine if one day you have more than 100 things on your "Gratitude List" or "Accomplishments List." That could be an extremely motivating and inspirational thing to look back on when you need some positive energy.

Strengths. Write down your personal strengths and positive attributes. Psychology shows us that we often have a "negativity bias" when it comes to thinking about ourselves; we tend to focus on our flaws rather than our strengths. So, think instead about the things you're good at. Start with just three to five positive characteristics about your-self (kind, smart, good listener, hardworking, etc.). Then try to think of at least one time when you embodied each characteristic. It could be something big or small, but the point is that you identify these posi-tive characteristics and recall times when you've demonstrated them. Reflecting on this list can instantly raise your confidence and sense of self-worth.

Accomplishments. Make a list of your past accomplishments. When we think about where we want to go in our lives and how we want to improve in the future, we often forget just how far we've already come. Everyone has experienced at least a few times when they've achieved something and were successful at something, big or small. Say you want to improve your math skills but haven't usually gotten good grades—except for the time you got an "A" in that high school class. Write that down under your accomplishments to remind yourself that you have the capacity to be good at math under the right circumstances. Past accomplishments can be a powerful motivation for future accomplishments, because they prove to us that we have the *potential* to be successful. In his book *Tools of Titans*, motivation guru Tim Ferriss recommends creating a "Jar of Awesome" filled with little pieces of paper on which you've written down past accomplishments Pick out a piece of paper at random whenever you need motivation and inspiration.

Gratitude. List things you are grateful for in your life. Your list can include very important things (like good health, a nice job, or a loving family) or much smaller things (spending time in the sun, walking in nature, enjoying your pet dog, listening to music). It's easy to focus on all of the things we don't have in our lives and forget the things we already have but take for granted. Psychology research is clear about the importance of "counting our blessings" and reflecting on what we have to be appreciative of in our lives, and how this contributes to happiness and mental health. One of the best ways to do this is to create a "Gratitude List" to reflect upon, especially when we are feeling down and need to remind ourselves that there is a lot of good in our lives.

To Do. Write a short list of the things you need to do. This is one of the most common and practical ways people use lists, and it can be an effective way to keep yourself focused and accountable. I recommend creating a daily "to do" list each night. This helps free your mind before sleep and lets you start the new day with a clear-cut plan. And it just feels good to go through your list and check things off! Start with the most important and urgent things; then you can add things that can be put off if you don't get to them. Jotting down three to five of the main things you need to do throughout your day is a simple but smart way to make sure you don't forget anything important.

Values. Write down your core life values. Our values are what should be driving most of our behaviors at a fundamental level, but sometimes we lose track of these priorities and end up focusing on things that don't really matter that much. This is a good exercise to help you identify what really gives your life meaning and purpose. Core values might include Family, Health, Religion, Safety, Education, Money, Fun/Pleasure. Make a list of your own main values and then see if you can rank them from most important to least important. This can give you a clearer idea about what you should focus on the most over the long term.

Music

Listening to music is one of the most common ways we have to change our moods and regulate our emotions. When we feel tired after a long day at work, many of us like to unwind by kicking back, closing our eyes, and turning on our iPods. Or when we feel down after a heated argument with a partner, we may use uplifting tunes to distract us from our anger or sadness. At this very moment I'm listening to some calm instrumental rock music, because it helps me stay relaxed and focused while I'm writing.

Music and Stress Relief

In one study done at the University of Gothenburg in 2012, participants who listened to music after stressful episodes in their everyday lives reported decreased stress compared to those who didn't listen to music in similar situations. In another study by the same team of researchers, music was found to be an effective way to reduce levels of cortisol, a hormone commonly released when we experience stress. This suggests that listening to music can have an actual biological effect on our mental health.

A growing body of research shows the benefits of music for lowering stress and anxiety levels. The next time you are feeling stressed out or overwhelmed, try lying down and listening to some favorite music. This can be a fine way to relax and rejuvenate yourself before you jump back into your day.

Music and Emotions

Music can serve many purposes when it comes to regulating our emotions and mental state. According to psychology researchers, these are the main ways we use music to manage our mental health and emotions:

- **Entertainment:** to maintain a positive mood or to evoke pleasure and positive emotions (joy, awe, humor).

- **Revival:** to relax and re-energize ourselves when we're feeling tired or stressed.

- **Diversion:** to distract ourselves from negative or undesirable thoughts.

- **Discharge:** to help us accept and release emotions such as anger or sadness.

- **Strong sensation:** to stimulate our senses in new ways and open our minds to new experiences.

- **Mental work:** to help us stay focused on completing a particular task, such as writing, programming, or other mental work.

- **Solace:** to experience comfort after a tragic or unfortunate event.

Naturally, what type of music you choose will depend on your personal musical preferences as well as what you want the music to do for you at a particular time. A study published in *Environment and Behavior* in 2004 showed that individuals who listened to "uplifting" music while working out at the gym (the researchers used hits by artists such as Madonna, Cher, The Corrs, and Blink-182) were more likely to push themselves compared to those listening to dissonant music (avant-garde composers such as Denis Smalley, James Dashow, and Stephen Kaske).

These findings make intuitive sense and ring true for me. Although I like some experimental and dissonant music, what works best for me while working out is music that is more upbeat, rhythmic, and (to me) inspiring. This doesn't mean that some types of music are better than others, just that different types are better for different purposes. If you want to relax, maybe you'll listen to a soothing classical composition. If you want to get pumped before a sports competition, fast techno or hip-hop may be better. And if you want to vent anger, heavy rock or metal might work for you.

Daily Listening

Here are a few ways we can use music to improve our psychology and well-being (along with some personal recommendations):

- An uplifting or inspiring song in the morning to help jump-start the day (e.g., Gorillaz—*Feel Good Inc.*)

- A relaxing or calming song after school or work to help relieve stress (e.g., Explosions in the Sky—*First Breath After Coma*)

- A fast or energetic song to motivate you to push yourself harder while working out at the gym (e.g., Led Zeppelin—*Immigrant Song*)

- Instrumental or classical music while doing homework or working on a task that requires thinking and problem-solving (e.g., Antonin Dvorak—*New World Symphony*)

- A song that makes you laugh to help turn around a bad mood (e.g., "Weird Al" Yankovic—*Amish Paradise*)

- A romantic or sexy song to help set the mood with a loved one (e.g., Marvin Gaye —*Let's Get It On*)

- Ambient or minimalist music to put you into a meditative and reflective state of mind (e.g., Steve Reich—*Music for 18 Musicians*)

- Experimental or avant-garde music to open your mind and stimulate your senses in new ways (e.g., Miles Davis—*Pharaoh's Dance*)

Some of my recommendations may not suit you, but they should give you a feeling for how different types of music can serve different functions. Build your own music playlists for different activities. You could have a "Motivation Playlist" for the gym, a "Focus Playlist" for work, and a "Relaxation Playlist" for nighttime listening, for example. Integrating more music into your daily routine can enhance almost any part of your life.

Role Models

Whether we realize it or not, we all have role models who influence who we are and whom we admire. As a social species, we are programmed to learn by observing others—seeing how they act and then mimicking what they do. This is a big part of how we learn as children, but as adults we often forget the power of having role models and continuing to learn from them.

A role model can be anyone you look up to in some way—parent, teacher, friend, scientist, athlete, actor/actress, religious leader, philosopher, celebrity, or even a fictional character from a movie, book, or TV show. If you ask any successful person, they'll likely be able to name role models who helped shape who they are and inspired them to be a better person. Maybe a professional baseball player looked up to a favorite player as a kid, an entrepreneur looked up to inventors and visionary thinkers, or a great dad was inspired by his own father.

Finding the right role models in your life can be an incredible source of positivity, inspiration, and motivation. It's not just about admiring people, but about using them to fuel your personal growth and transformation. Role models can be a resource to help improve any personality trait (humor, intelligence, kindness) or skill (good conversationalist, music ability, athletic ability etc.).

In my experience, choosing role models is one of the most important exercises in self-improvement. I have a "Role Models" document on my computer that I've been revisiting and updating for more than five years now. It's a wonderful source of inspiration.

Here's a small sampling from my "Role Models" list:

Confidence: George Clooney, Joe Rogan, Johnny Depp, James Bond, Gene Simmons, Denzel Washington, Kanye West

Intelligence: Carl Sagan, Steven Pinker, Charles Darwin, Albert Einstein, Neil deGrasse Tyson, Raymond Kurzweil, Daniel Dennett, Marvin Minsky, Douglas Hofstadter

Humor: Robin Williams, Dave Chappelle, Doug Stanhope, Norm MacDonald, Zach Galifianakis, Stephen Colbert, George Carlin, Bill Hicks, Aziz Ansari

Creativity: David Lynch, Frank Zappa, Charlie Kaufman, Quentin Tarantino, Alex Grey, Salvador Dali, Coen Brothers, Pixar, Steven Spielberg, Tim Burton

Kindness: Buddha, Dalai Lama, Mother Teresa, Gandhi, Martin Luther King Jr., Carl Rogers

Work ethic: Steve Jobs, Gary Vaynerchuk, Mike Patton, Henry Rollins, Lee Kuan Yew, David Wright

Of course, this list is personal to me. Your list should include role models that are meaningful to you. You can break down your list in a way that suits your own values and goals. If you want to focus on "Health," for instance, list people who embody health and fitness. Include role models who are family members, friends, or other real-world acquaintances. I omitted these from my sample because their names wouldn't mean anything to you.

Learning from other individuals isn't about trying to copy or mimic their every move. In the end, you have to be *yourself*. But that doesn't mean you can't learn a thing or two from someone else along the way. And having people you admire doesn't mean that you worship everything about them. People are usually a mixed bag of positive and negative characteristics. When choosing a role model, you are focusing on what you like about that person. If you want to learn how to be a boxer, watch videos of Mike Tyson, but that doesn't mean you have to take relationship advice from him.

Making the Most of Your Role Models

Role models can be a huge part of any self-improvement effort. Take the time to find individuals who really inspire you to keep moving forward with your goals, whatever they may be. Often the best role models are those whose goals are similar to ours. Make sure you pay attention to their struggles and failures, as that can give you a more practical view of what it takes to be successful—and teach you that your role models didn't always have it easy.

Make a list of role models. Identify a trait or skill you want to work on, then try to list at least three role models who embody that trait or skill for you. It's fine to identify multiple traits or skills and list role models for each of them (as I did above). Then save your list in your self-improvement folder. This can be an excellent resource to go back to and continue to build on.

Do research on your role models. Learn as much about your role models as possible to find out what makes them tick and why they are successful. Search for quotes, articles, images, and/or videos. I love watching interviews with successful people, because I see it as an awesome opportunity to learn something new that I can apply to my life. You can save these resources with your "List of Role Models" so you always have a way to find a special quote, article, or video that inspires you.

Imagine a situation from their perspective. One of the best ways to learn from your role models is to ask yourself, "What would _____ do in this situation?" By looking at a situation from another person's viewpoint, we can gain insight into new ways of thinking, feeling, and behaving. Just identify a situation in your life that you want to improve on, find a role model who is successful in similar situations, and try to imagine how you would act if you were that person. By doing this, we become aware of the different responses we might choose in a given circumstance, often different from the way we would typically respond.

Ask them questions. If you have the chance, simply talk to your role models directly and ask them questions. This is a good option for people you know in real life (family, friends, coworkers), but you can also reach out to successful people you don't actually know. I'm often surprised by the caliber of people who respond to my questions (through email or social media) if I simply make the effort to reach out to them. Most experts love showing off their expertise, so asking questions and becoming interested in their work often pleases them, and they are more than happy to give advice. Pick your role model's brains to find out what makes them tick and why they are successful at what they do.

Write an essay about your role model. Once you've done research on a particular role model, you probably have enough information at your disposal to write a short essay about them. This may sound like homework, but it's a good way to solidify what you've learned and make it stick in your brain. Writing a 500- to 700-word essay can help you identify the key lessons you've picked up from your role model. Try to answer these questions: "What do I admire most about this person? What struggles did my role model face and how did he or she overcome them? How can I apply what I've learned to my own life?"

Vision Boards

A vision board is a way to dedicate space in your home or office to motivational purposes. All you have to do is get yourself some cork board or poster board and fill it up with images, goals, affirmations, and other positive words that embody your core values and goals in life.

The process of creating a vision board is, in itself, a motivating activity that can give you a clearer picture of where you want to go in life and what you aim to achieve. Once it's finished, your board becomes a fantastic daily reminder of what drives you in life.

It's not much different from the way an aspiring athlete has posters of favorite players all over their bedroom walls, or an aspiring singer decorates with photographs and lyrics from favorite bands, or a would-be filmmaker puts up movie quotes and film posters. When you create a vision board and hang it up, it becomes a symbolic space for positivity, inspiration, and motivation.

 **exercise**
Creating a Vision Board of Your Own

STEP **1.** Start by finding a cork board or poster board that you can fit somewhere on a wall at home or in your office. You can buy these online or at your local office supply or art supply store.

STEP **2.** Gather paper, scissors, pins, markers, tape, glue, or whatever else you might need to put together your vision board.

STEP **3.** Review your affirmations and quotes, role model list, and motivational lists to find ideas for the types of things you may want to include on your vision board.

STEP **4.** Look through magazines or newspapers or search online to find images or phrases that strike a chord with you. Cut out the ones you want to integrate into your vision board or print images from your computer.

STEP **5.** Once you have all of your materials and a good idea of what sort of vision board you want to create, schedule a day to create your vision board. Add music to enrich the experience or get together with a friend to make vision boards.

STEP **6.** Consider adding a "Daily Actions" section. Vision boards are nice for helping you think about the bigger picture, but they shouldn't distract you from taking daily action. Add a list of small actions to help you think practically and productively.

STEP **7.** Experiment. Be creative. Think of your vision board as an art project, and try to make it unique in a way that suits your personality. There's no right or wrong way to create one—it's all up to you.

STEP **8.** Keep it evolving. After you finish your vision board you can add or subtract things whenever you feel like it. When you discover an inspiring image or article, find space to add it to your board.

STEP **9.** You might choose to create a whole new vision board at the beginning of each year, especially if some of your core goals and values have changed. Nothing is carved in stone; this is just a tool to get your mind thinking in the right directions.

Vision boards provide a fun opportunity to give yourself a daily injection of motivation and inspiration. They can be incredibly powerful for some people. I've used them a lot when I've wanted to make drastic shifts in my perspective.

Social Networks

The people we surround ourselves with on a daily basis have a huge impact on how we live our lives. As the saying goes, "Show me your five closest friends and I'll show you your future."

Psychology research supports this axiom. According to the book *Connected: The Surprising Power of Our Social Networks and How They Shape Our Lives* by Nicholas Christakis and James Fowler, studies show that if you hang around people who are overweight and unhealthy then you're more likely to be overweight and unhealthy yourself, and if you hang around people who don't do their homework or study for exams you're likely to have poorer grades. We become a reflection of the kinds of people we spend the most time with. This social influence affects every area of our lives: at home, at work, at school, at a party, or wherever.

Think about your own personal goals and values. Are there any people in your life who are currently holding you back from achieving your goals? Be honest. Instead of spending a lot of time with people who make you hate life and want to give up on your goals, spend time with people who make you love life and motivate you to improve yourself.

To me, this is one of the most important characteristics in a healthy relationship. It's also essential for achieving success. If you have the right people in your life, it will be easy to find that extra shot of motivation and support when you really need it.

We may like to believe that we can change all by ourselves, without help from anyone, but this actually limits our ability to grow and improve. It's crucial that we have supportive family members or friends to help bring out the best versions of ourselves. Besides having an unconscious influence on us, they can hold us accountable for our actions and give us guidance and motivation during difficult times in our development.

Building a Powerful Social Network

Don't underestimate the importance of finding the right people to help motivate you, inspire you, and hold you accountable to your goals and ambitions. They are out there, waiting to help you.

Find people who are better than you. One of the most helpful things you can do is to find someone who has already been successful at what you are trying to accomplish. You don't have to consider them better than you as a person, just in this particular area. Try to surround yourself with people who are smarter and more successful than you in different ways. Being around them will help bring out the best in you. No matter where you are in life, there are always others you can learn from. Be open to finding and building relationships with those people. Perhaps you can already identify some of them from your Role Models list. Spend time with them, and their good habits will start to rub off on you.

Find people who have similar goals. It's important that your social network includes someone who shares similar goals with you. If you and a friend both want to lose weight, or read more books, or start a business, then you can hold each other accountable and motivate each other. You could even make a pact that you will always go to the gym together on certain days, or read the same book each week and talk about it, or report back monthly on your business earnings and share tips. A simple pact with a friend can be highly motivating—you don't want to let your friends down, so you're not just doing something for yourself but also for someone else you like. That can provide a powerful extra incentive to stick to your goals.

Find online forums and message boards. It's not always easy to find people who share our goals and ambitions. Thankfully, we now have the whole internet available to help us connect with people we would never have had access to in the past. In fact, there's a forum or message board dedicated to virtually any type of passion, hobby, or interest you might have. These online communities are often filled with helpful people answering each other's questions and sharing unique advice. Reddit is one place I frequently use to connect with people. They have whole communities dedicated to health, dating, relationships, meditation, productivity, entrepreneurship, and anything else related to self-improvement that you can think of. You may have to do some searching before you find an online community that fits you, but there's definitely one out there. Online communities can be valuable supplements or substitutes if you don't have many supportive relationships in the real world.

Create a positive social media feed. Another way to use the internet is to create a social media account completely dedicated to positivity, motivation, and self-improvement. This can be done on platforms such as Twitter, Facebook, Tumblr, or Instagram. While there can be a lot of negativity on social media (arguing about politics, religion, news, or whatever), there can also be a lot of positivity. Fill your social media feed with positive people and avoid/block negative people. This is at least one corner of our lives where we have direct control over whom we interact with. You don't need to do this with your personal accounts, but at least one social media account dedicated to nothing but self-improvement can be a great idea. Find people who share positive articles, tips, quotes, images, and the like so that you have a constant source of new inspiration. There are also many famous and successful people on social media who can be insightful and informative.

Don't be afraid to ask for help. We often think of asking for help as a sign of weakness, or something to be ashamed of, but the truth is that asking for help when we really need it can be a great strength. There's no need to reinvent the wheel all on your own. The most successful people stand on the shoulders of giants and learn from others to build the best version of themselves. Why try to figure everything out on your own when you have people who can guide you in the right direction so that you can get where you want to go more quickly? When you find yourself around smart and successful people, don't hesitate to pick their brains and see if they have any good advice for you. The more willing you are to ask for help, the more you'll learn from others and the more you'll grow as a person. There's nothing wrong with admitting that you're not perfect and don't know everything. That's not a weakness, that's a strength.

Join real-world clubs and meetups. Another way to reach out to new people in your community and build up your social network is to search for local clubs, meetups, or organizations that you can join. For example, if you want to be healthier, then think about joining a basketball league, yoga class, or rock-climbing club. Or if you want to work on your business, look for a local mastermind group or Toastmasters club, or take a business class at a nearby college. It may be difficult to find some of these, depending on where you live, but keep your eyes and ears open and do some research. Remember, if you make one good friend, that can lead to being introduced to all of their friends as well. It only takes one new connection to open up a whole new social network of friends.

Find one person who holds you accountable. Sometimes we can be our own worst enemies, especially when we fill our heads with lies, excuses, pessimism, and negativity. This kind of thinking can keep us stuck in a negative cycle, which is why it's crucial that we have friends who can call us out on our lies and excuses. Such a person is a rare but valuable friend. For the sake of being polite, most people don't challenge their friends this way. And while no one wants to be around someone who's constantly criticizing and nitpicking, a huge part of self-improvement is having at least one friend who is willing to be 100 percent honest with you and tell it like it is—especially when you ask for feedback. Often, a close friend can understand us better than we understand ourselves, and when people look at us from an outside perspective they can have insights that we don't pick up on our own. It's hard to do, but be willing to listen to constructive criticism and feedback. Pay extra attention to those things you take personally—that can be the most revealing about what you need to work on but may be avoiding.

Small Steps: Relationships

- Say "Hi" to others when you cross paths
- Say "Please" and "Thank you" (even for small things)
- Be a good listener, giving people time to speak without interruption
- Make eye contact when speaking with people
- Smile more frequently
- Give at least one compliment to someone each day
- Treat everyone with respect, regardless of social status
- Make sure that less-outgoing people feel included and heard
- Be aware of your tone of voice
- Don't talk too loudly in public places
- Put away your phone when talking to people
- Show up on time—don't keep others waiting on you
- Treat professional servers with respect

- Don't talk behind people's backs

- Avoid nitpicking over other people's mistakes

- Minimize discussion on heated topics

- If someone embarrasses themselves during a conversation, try to change the subject

- Apologize and admit when you're wrong

- Stay in touch with old friends and family, even if it's just with a text message

- Be honest about your thoughts and feelings without being aggressive

- Learn to let others have the last word

- Respect your elders; listen to them and learn from their stories

- Write a personal letter to show someone you care

- Introduce people to one another

- If you have criticism for someone, express it to them in private

- Try to see things from the other person's perspective before passing judgment

- Don't make jokes at someone else's expense

- Give firm handshakes when meeting new people

- Forgive and let go when others hurt or disappoint you

- Give people space when they need it

- Be open to feedback from others without taking it personally

- Reflect on the positive experiences you've had with people

Imagination and Mental Rehearsal

Ultimately, all self-change is about seeing yourself in new ways. This is why your imagination can be a powerful tool for changing your thoughts, feelings, and behaviors.

Neuroscience research has revealed that when we imagine ourselves doing a particular thing, it activates many of the same regions in our brains as when we are physically doing that same thing. This is strong evidence that "mental rehearsal" can be a useful way to condition ourselves toward new and more desirable behaviors.

Basically, the more we visualize ourselves doing an activity, the stronger the neural connections associated with that habit. The more these neural firings occur, the more likely they are to undergo *long-term potentiation*, a cellular process that underlies all learning and memory. After the neural associations are successfully built, they become a natural reaction in the brain. Then when we are presented with a situation similar to the one we've imagined, we're more likely to act out the habits we trained ourselves to do during our mental rehearsal.

This doesn't mean we can learn new habits simply by imagining ourselves doing them. Real-world practice still matters. But mental rehearsal can be a valuable way to build habits faster and make them stronger.

Many athletes, actors, musicians, and other performers use visualization as a type of mental rehearsal. They imagine themselves acting out a situation step by step, and that prepares them for when it's finally time to take the field or hit the stage. A professional golfer will visualize a putt multiple times before taking the shot, or a professional actor will rehearse his lines inside his head before he hits the stage. A professional concert pianist will imagine herself playing a piece before a big performance.

Practicing Mental Rehearsal

Of all the tools mentioned in this chapter, mental rehearsal can be one of the hardest to master—but if you practice it often enough, it can be one of the most powerful tools at your disposal. Once you reach that point, it becomes nearly effortless to see yourself thinking, feeling, and acting in new ways.

Choose a habit you want to change. First identify a specific habit that you are trying to change. Say you want to stop drinking when you go out to parties, but every time you end up at a party you can't seem to help yourself. Or you want to go to the gym more regularly, but when you wake up in the morning you just can't seem to bring yourself to go. Find situations that seem too difficult to change when you're in the moment and mentally rehearse the new habits you want to adopt, *before* you find yourself in those situations again.

Find a quiet place and close your eyes. Before mental rehearsal, find a quiet place where you can close your eyes and really focus on your imagination. Try to limit external distractions so that you can be fully engaged in the experience. Put on your headphones and listen to relaxing music, if that helps. Take a few deep breaths to put yourself into a calm state before you begin your mental rehearsal.

Imagine situations from everyday life. When starting your mental rehearsal, try to imagine yourself in a place from your everyday life. Paint a picture in your head and look around. Imagine yourself in your actual home or office, or wherever. Point out some everyday things: "There's my bed," "There's my desk," "There's my plant," and so on. This will help make the visualization more real to you, which will prepare your mind to recognize the situation in the real world.

Visualize each step of the process. The most important aspect of mental rehearsal is to visualize the entire process, step by step. If you're trying to build the habit of going to the gym in the morning, start your visualization from the moment you get out of bed. See yourself going through each step of your morning: taking a shower, getting dressed, eating breakfast, getting into your car, driving to the gym, going inside, running on the treadmill, lifting weights, and, finally, walking out of the gym. The more detailed you are in your mental rehearsal, the easier it will be to walk through these same steps in real life. The whole mental rehearsal process shouldn't take any longer than 5 or 10 minutes, but for maximum effect it's important that you imagine yourself acting out each step of the habit you want build.

Evoke multiple senses. When people think about mental rehearsal, they usually think of sight and visualization, but it's helpful to evoke your other senses as well—sound, touch, smell, and taste. Imagine what these senses may be experiencing in the situation you're visualizing. For example, ask yourself, "What type of sounds do I usually hear at the gym?" or "How does my body feel running on the treadmill or lifting weights?"—or even "How does the gym usually smell?" You don't need to get bogged down in the details, but evoking multiple senses will help to make your rehearsal more realistic, and it will help to fix the habit in your mind.

End on a positive note. No matter what habit you are trying to build, try to find a way to end your rehearsal on a positive note. For example, imagine yourself walking out of the gym with an upright posture, feeling confident about yourself. It helps to imagine some sort of immediate reward, even if it's just feeling good about yourself. Relish those positive feelings for a bit, and carry that positive energy and inspiration with you once you open your eyes.

Play pretend, have fun! Remember, the whole point of this exercise is to use your imagination to help change your thoughts, feelings, and behaviors. There are no limitations to how you can use your imagination, so be willing to play pretend and experiment. Do whatever makes you feel more positive, motivated, and energized. Try exaggerating your actions, having fun, or being silly. Imagine yourself as a superhero. Imagine positive energy surrounding you. Imagine yourself being super strong. The more fun you have with your mental rehearsal, the more likely it will stick with you and have a real impact on your mind. Used the right way, imagination can be one of the most powerful ways to change our minds.

Practice and patience are important. When you first try mental rehearsal, it may seem a bit weird, awkward, or unnatural. Most people aren't used to using their imaginations actively this way. And when you first try to visualize something, it's likely going to be a bit blurry. If you have trouble visualizing at first, just *pretend* that you know how to do it. Try your best and go through the process. It may take multiple sessions before your imagination begins to improve—it's no different from a muscle that needs to be exercised in order to be strengthened. You'll probably need to repeat the process a few times before you notice a significant change in your thoughts, feelings, and behaviors.

CHAPTER SEVEN

Stress, Relaxation, and Healthy Breaks

Stress is a normal part of our existence. It is best defined as a physical and mental response to any type of threat or demand in our environment. We all experience some stress when we are challenged by the never-ending obstacles we face in our lives, whether at work, at school, at home, or wherever.

The truth is, life isn't completely easy for anyone, and we can't expect to be relaxed and comfortable all the time. We all have things we'd rather not have to deal with or that we don't have much control over—and that's where much of our stress comes from.

Biologist Robert Sapolsky is one of the leading researchers on stress. He says that stress is a natural and adaptive response of our nervous system, fueled by two hormones—epinephrine (adrenaline) and norepinephrine. These are evolutionarily designed to be released in our bodies when we perceive a potential danger or threat in our environment. The release of these hormones creates a biological response known as the "fight or flight or freeze" response. This heightened state of arousal makes us super-energized and focused.

If an animal is feeling threatened by a predator, it will engage in one of three main responses:

- Fight—Attack the predator

- Flight—Run away from the predator

- Freeze—Stop moving or play dead

Today we still respond to stress in similar ways. However, now the threat isn't usually a predator but a deadline to meet at work, an argument with a friend, or a class in which we're doing poorly.

The stress in our lives can be a good thing, but if it becomes excessive it can have negative effects on both our physical and our mental health. High levels of stress are associated with loss of focus, diminished cognitive abilities, and difficulty learning new things, as well as low energy and fatigue, higher susceptibility to sickness and illness (including heart disease and cancer), and even shorter lifespans.

Learning how to handle the stress in your life is essential to maximizing your happiness, health, and well-being. This chapter will talk about what we can do to manage stress more effectively, no matter what the source of that stress may be.

Reframing the Fight, Flight, or Freeze Response

The first step in becoming smarter about your stress is reframing the "fight or flight or freeze" response as something positive. This requires that we a) recognize when stress is actually a signal we can use to guide our lives and b) learn how to respond appropriately to stress in certain situations.

In the right doses, stress can be helpful. We've evolved to have the "fight or flight or freeze" response for practical reasons, and in many ways those reasons still apply, just in a different form. While today's stress is not usually caused by challenges that are directly life threatening, it does often direct our focus toward problems that need attention. Here's how to reframe your stress responses to address those problems:

Reframing "fight." Stress can motivate you to focus on your problems and take active measures to face and fix them. For example, feeling stressed out about an exam can motivate you to study harder to make sure you do well.

Reframing "flight." Stress can help you identify problems that you may want to reduce or eliminate from your life. For example, if a certain person at work stresses you out, you can try to minimize the time you spend talking to that individual.

Reframing "freeze." Stress can cause you to take a step back and reevaluate a situation before going back to it. If you're feeling stressed out about your job, for example, you may want to reflect on how much that job really means to you and whether it's worth it to stay.

General Adaptation Syndrome

Stress can be caused by any stimulus—real or imagined—that we perceive as a threat. According to pioneering biologist Hans Selye, this then triggers a physical response in our bodies known as "general adaptation syndrome." This includes three main stages:

- Alarm: Our bodies go into a heightened state of arousal in which we become super-alert and focused.

- Resistance: We search for ways to respond and combat the stressful stimulus until it is no longer bothering us.

- Exhaustion: Our bodies become tired and need to take a break to relax and re-energize.

The "alarm" stages make us aware of the stress, the "resistance" stage motivates us to take action, and the "exhaustion" stage is what we experience after depleting our physical and mental resources. Here's a diagram that illustrates our ability to cope with stress during these three stages:

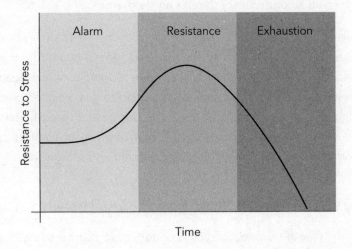

As you can see, by the exhaustion stage our ability to manage stress falls dramatically. And long-term exposure to this exhaustion stage can make us tired and weaken our immune system so that we easily become sick and depressed. When we enter this stage, we need to find ways to step back, relax, and rejuvenate our bodies and minds before we jump back into a stressful activity.

In Defense of Your Comfort Zone

In self-improvement literature, you'll see a lot of advice about "going outside of your comfort zone." Your comfort zone is typically seen as playing it safe. It's when you choose comfort, familiarity, and security rather than novelty, risk-taking, and challenging yourself.

In many ways, it's a good thing to step outside of your comfort zone and challenge yourself. We can't grow or evolve without doing this. But your comfort zone can also get an unnecessarily bad reputation.

It's not something that needs to be completely avoided. In fact, your comfort zone plays an integral role in your self-improvement, because it gives you an opportunity to relax and recharge.

Going outside your comfort zone comes with costs—it can be stressful and demand a great deal of physical and mental energy from you. Constantly pushing yourself outside your comfort zone can lead to frustration and fatigue. Sometimes you need to give yourself permission to take it easy and "chill out." You don't need to push yourself forward every second of the day. This is where your comfort zone becomes a valuable tool for self-improvement and self-growth.

Pay Attention to Your Sensitivity Threshold

Pushing yourself outside of your comfort zone can be stressful and challenging. It's not easy—it takes work.

When I expose myself to viewpoints I don't agree with or try things that I've never done before, it takes a lot of energy out of me, especially if those experiences don't match with my usual personality. I'm introverted and reserved—I don't like super-busy and loud clubs or dance parties. I don't mind going to one every now and then, but it takes energy out of me because it's not in my usual comfort zone. Everyone engages in some activities that fit within their comfort zone and others that don't. These may be influenced both by our individual personalities and by our past experiences.

The key to managing your comfort zone is to identify when you've hit your *sensitivity threshold*. Your sensitivity threshold is the amount of discomfort you can handle before an experience becomes toxic and damaging. Experiencing discomfort in moderate doses can be healthy and rewarding, but once we've passed our sensitivity threshold it's time to retreat to our comfort zone and recharge ourselves.

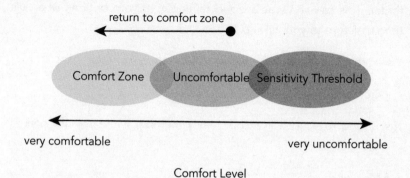

Comfort Level

Self-improvement requires a delicate balance between going outside your comfort zone and recognizing when it's time to go back to your comfort zone. This is an important principle for managing the stress levels in your life.

Just as everyone's comfort zone is different, so is everyone's sensitivity threshold. Some people can experience a great deal of discomfort before it becomes too much, while others may only be able to bear a small amount. Identifying your own sensitivity threshold is crucial for managing the stress and anxiety in your life. What are the situations in which you typically become the most stressed?

What Does Your Comfort Zone Look Like?

Do you know what your comfort zone looks like? What activities or situations allow you to step back, relax, and recharge your batteries? You want to have a clear picture of your comfort zone so that you know what options you have when you find yourself becoming over-whelmed with life.

Maybe your comfort zone entails surrounding yourself with family and friends. Or maybe it's about spending time by yourself, reading a book, playing video games, or going for a walk. I recommend making a list of 10 or so "Relaxation Activities" to save in your self-improvement folder. This can serve as a good reminder of your options when it's time to return to your comfort zone.

Here are some ideas from my own "Relaxation Activities" list:

- Going for a walk outside
- Talking to a close friend or family member (write specific names on your list)
- Making music
- Listening to music
- Reading a book
- Playing a video game
- Watching a movie or TV show
- Meditating
- Writing poetry
- Playing with my dog

What you put on *your* list will depend on you and your personality. Focus on small activities that can function as 15- to 45-minute breaks, especially things that you can easily integrate into your daily schedule.

It's good to have a list like this so that you have multiple options when you need to step back and relax. You'll likely be in the mood for different kinds of breaks at different times, so it's helpful to have different choices available to you.

In Dave Crenshaw's practical and insightful book *The Power of Having Fun: How Meaningful Breaks Help You Get More Done*, he highlights the importance of scheduling time for relaxation throughout the day. Crenshaw uses the metaphor of walking through a desert and needing to stop at an oasis for rejuvenation.

Depending on the activity, most people can only focus on work for 45 to 90 minutes at a stretch before they start getting tired and distracted. It's important to schedule mini-breaks throughout the day to keep energy levels high and both body and mind refreshed. Relaxation plays an important role in our overall productivity, so it's crucial to balance stressful activities with relaxation. This means taking breaks from your work whenever it's appropriate and necessary.

When you reach the point in your day when you just can't seem to focus on work, it's probably time to walk away, get a breath of fresh air, or have a friendly chat with someone—whatever gives your body and mind a temporary break so you can go back to work with a renewed outlook.

Building Relaxation into Your Day

If you want to master the stress in your life, know when it's time to embrace stressful and challenging activities and when it's time to take a step back and relax for a bit. The balancing point is going to be different for each individual, but when you discover where that balance is for you, you'll maximize both your productivity and your happiness.

Identify what times you get tired. Our days tend to follow a predictable routine—we feel more energized at certain times of the day, less energized at other times. It's common to experience a slump in the middle of the afternoon, for instance. Our days typically have a particular flow to them—take note of when you feel the most tired. That's probably when you need to schedule a break in order to reboot.

Find what breaks work best for you. Different kinds of breaks are going to work better for you than others, depending on your personality and the type of work you do. Someone who does physical labor all day may benefit from breaks that involve sitting down, reading a book, or engaging in some sort of mental activity. But someone who works in an office or does mental labor may benefit more from taking a walk. Try to find breaks that help balance out your work rather than depending on the same skills. Otherwise, your breaks may sap more of your energy rather than letting you rest.

Create a "Relaxation Activities" list. As mentioned above, regarding understanding your comfort zone, I strongly urge you to write out a short "Relaxation Activities" list with at least 10 activities that you find calming and relaxing. While you may find it obvious to identify what relaxes you, it really helps to write it down and save it so that you are aware of all the choices you have. Save this list in your self-improvement folder and add new activities as you think of them. The more options you have, the easier it will be to integrate relaxation into your day.

The power of short and long breaks. The length of your breaks really depends on how much you need to re-energize. Sometimes just getting up for five minutes is all you need in order to refocus. When you hit your midday slump, an hour-long lunch break may be appropriate. At other times you may need a much longer break to get yourself back in the groove, maybe a "mental health day" or even a week's vacation. Short breaks (up to 15 minutes), medium breaks (an hour or two), and long breaks (a day or longer) can all play important roles in keeping our minds fresh.

Reflect on your daily routine. Look back on your daily routine. Remember the exercise from Chapter 1 and ask yourself, "What relaxation activities can I add to my schedule? And what are the best times to do them?" It's healthy to dedicate specific times throughout your day to relaxing and having fun. And writing relaxation into your daily schedule will help you to feel less guilty when you first step away from work. Make relaxation a natural part of your day.

Take a break when you're really stuck. If your work requires a great deal of creativity or problem-solving, you may frequently find yourself bogged down on a particular problem. It's tempting to keep racking our brains and pushing ourselves to find a solution, but sometimes the best thing to do is to walk away from the problem for a little while. By taking a break, we let our minds work at the problem on an unconscious level. That can lead to insights we wouldn't find if we tried to approach the problem directly. It also allows us to go back to work with a new perspective. There are many times when I take a break from trying to write a song, and then when I go back to it the creativity starts flowing more spontaneously.

Relaxation isn't laziness! Society often emphasizes the value of keeping busy or doing something productive. We think of relaxation as something that's lazy or a waste of time—but that couldn't be further from the truth. Society's smartest and hardest workers are those who know how to take a break when it really counts. If you don't, you actually become less productive; you're tiring yourself out so that you can't work to the best of your ability. Always remember that relaxation and productivity are two sides of the same coin.

The Power of Leisure and Hobbies

I've focused on why leisure and relaxation are important for minimizing stress and increasing focus and energy, but there are other benefits that are worth touching on here. Leisure activities can boost many positive emotions and raise our overall sense of happiness and well-being. Here are some ways leisure can make our lives better:

Recovery. Leisure provides a way to relax and recover after working. This helps us avoid fatigue and burnout, which can hamper both happiness and productivity. Working 24/7 isn't actually the best way to be productive. You need to balance knowing when to push yourself forward against knowing when to take a step back. Leisure allows us to take time off from our major responsibilities and detach for a little while.

Autonomy. Leisure can create a sense of choice and autonomy. Our work and responsibilities may be dictated by others, but pursuing hobbies during our free time gives us a greater sense of control over our lives. Our free time may be one of the few areas in our lives that is self-directed and self-determined. That helps to relieve stress and anxiety and gives us a sense of power over our own lives.

Mastery. Leisure can cultivate a healthy sense of personal success and accomplishment. Though we enjoy our hobbies, many of them require effort and skill to master, whether we're solving sudoku puzzles or writing poetry, making music, or playing a video game. No one can be good at everything, but everyone can be good at *something*. That's an important psychological need to which we should all pay attention. Find enjoyable activities that let you show progress, improved skill, or some level of achievement and mastery. Completing small goals for fun—making progress in *anything*—can be a nice boost in confidence and self-esteem that can then spill over into other areas of life.

Meaning. Leisure can be a source of meaning and purpose. Many activities and hobbies hold personal significance to us and to the bigger picture behind our lives. For example, activities we like to do in our free time may be tied to a religious or spiritual tradition (going to church, volunteering, working with a charity or nonprofit). Or leisure activities may have meaning because they play a sentimental role in our lives: Maybe you like to play the guitar because your dad taught you how to play, or you like to play baseball because you played in high school. The things we choose to do in our free time can be sentimental, nostalgic, and meaningful, adding an extra layer of positivity to our lives.

Socializing. Leisure time gives us an opportunity to connect with people and be more social. While many hobbies can be done either alone or with other people, spending some of your leisure time being social can provide an important sense of friendship, community, and belonging. Such activities might include joining a weekend sports league or a monthly book club, playing a multiplayer video game with friends, or just going to a restaurant or bar with good people. During our free time, we have greater choice over what people we surround ourselves with, so it's good to schedule time with friends we really enjoy.

Do Your Leisure Activities Meet All Your Needs?

The potential benefits offered by leisure activities provide a good guideline for determining how effectively you are spending your free time. For example, if you mostly spend your free time watching TV, that may help with the "recovery" aspect of leisure, but is it fulfilling your "mastery" needs, or your "meaning" or "social" needs? Probably not.

When you think about your usual leisure activities, do you feel like all your needs are being fulfilled? If not, it might be a good idea to introduce some new activities and hobbies into your routine. Try to have a wide range of leisure activities to fulfill multiple needs. Maybe some days you just want to sit at home and play the guitar by yourself, but some nights it's better to go out to a restaurant or bar with friends.

While many of us lead busy lives, it's still important to carve out time for relaxation. According to the book *168 Hours: You Have More Time Than You Think* by Laura Vanderkam, we tend to overestimate our commitments each week and underestimate how much time we have to ourselves, especially the time we could spend doing activities we actually enjoy. Most people should be able to find some time to simply relax and engage in pleasurable activities.

If you truly find it impossible to find time in your day for relaxation or leisure, that likely means you have way too much on your plate and your current daily routine is unsustainable in the long term. Don't underestimate the importance of letting yourself relax. Make sure your relaxation and leisure needs are being met daily. This is essential for building a happier and healthier lifestyle.

Small Steps: Mental Health

- Make time in your day for relaxation

- Pursue a creative hobby

- Spend time around positive people

- Write about past mistakes and failures to learn from them

- Write about your individual strengths and past accomplishments

- Listen to music to change your mood

- Minimize your exposure to negative information

- Focus on what's in your power to change

- Take a nature walk once per week

- Practice mindfulness meditation once per week

- Make a list of the things for which you are grateful

- Read two books each year that expand your perspective

- Do one kind deed each day—with no expectation of anything in return

- Find ways to give to your community and help others by volunteering your time and resources

- Spend more time kissing, hugging, and cuddling

- Believe in something bigger than yourself

- Take a "mental health day" when you really need it

- Make a list of your core values in life

- Find an activity that gives you a sense of purpose

- Find 10 minutes each day to smile, sing, or dance

- Try to find the humor in things and laugh more

- If it's part of your belief system, pray more often

===========================

CHAPTER EIGHT

Nighttime Ritual: End Every Day on the Right Note

How you end each day is just as important as how you start each day.

We've already covered the importance of creating a morning ritual that energizes you before you jump into your day. Now we'll focus on creating a nighttime ritual so that you can end your day on the right note as well.

We should start every morning with a kick in the behind and end every night with a pat on the back. Mornings are when you should build up your energy, get yourself motivated, and be ready to conquer your day. Nighttimes are when you should slow down, reflect on your day, and prepare yourself for rest.

If you look back on your daily routine exercise from Chapter 1, you can probably already find some type of nighttime ritual that you typically follow. Even something as simple as flipping on the TV, watching cartoons while lying in bed, and eating potato chips until you pass out can be considered a type of nighttime ritual, albeit not the healthiest one.

When we approach nighttime, we're likely to feel worn out from all of the work we've been doing throughout the day. This makes it easy to engage in unhealthy behaviors, because our willpower is often running low and we just want to relax. While relaxation should be part of any nighttime ritual, we need to do this in a healthy and productive way that feeds our overall values and goals.

Your Own Nighttime Ritual

Most people define their "nighttime" as beginning sometime after they eat dinner. For others, it may be a bit later—maybe "once the kids go to bed." However you define the beginning of your night, the aim of your nighttime ritual is to wrap up your day and prepare yourself to go to sleep. This will likely begin one to three hours before you plan to go to bed.

Let me start by describing my own nighttime ritual, and what function each activity serves for me:

- **Eat dinner.** Typically, my work-related day ends around dinner time, so I usually consider this the beginning of my night.

- **Wash dishes/clean something.** After I've eaten, I usually do a 15-minute cleanup, especially in the kitchen. This is a simple and productive activity that can be calming when you're in the right mindset—and it's always healthiest not to leave any household mess lingering for too long.

- **Check emails.** I'll check my email one last time to make sure I haven't missed anything important. This way I can fully let go of work for the rest of the night.

- **Make a quick "to do" list for tomorrow.** I'll spend a couple of minutes jotting down the main tasks I need to accomplish the next day. I usually do this in a small notepad I keep on my desk. This is another thing that helps me to let go of work for the rest of the night. It also saves me from lying in bed thinking about what I need to do tomorrow.

- **Watch TV/play video games.** This is the part of my day when I really start winding down and de-stressing. Depending on my mood, I'll watch a movie I've been wanting to check out or a TV show I've been following, or I'll play a video game. I typically spend a solid hour or two this way, but on weekend nights I might stretch it out to three or four hours. This is a key time in my day to have fun and temporarily let go of work and responsibilities.

- **Have a glass of wine.** Often I'll have a glass of wine (or a shot of whiskey) while I'm watching a movie or playing a video game. Of course, this is *my* routine, and I don't necessarily suggest it for anyone else (especially if you have problems with drinking), but for me this is a relatively harmless pleasure.

- **Gaze at the stars.** I love spending time with nature, and even just going outside and staring up at the sky for a bit can be a really nice, relaxing, and introspective experience. Night skies are particularly beautiful when it's clear out and you can see the moon and stars. I only need 15 minutes or less outside on any given night to receive a small surge of awe and gratitude—a wonderful feeling to have at the end of the day.

- **Brush teeth/wash face.** This is typical getting ready for bed stuff, but I make sure to brush my teeth and wash my face so that I feel clean and fresh when my head hits the pillow. I usually take the opportunity to feed myself some positive thoughts while I'm doing these things.

- **Reflect on what I'm grateful for.** Usually while brushing my teeth, I'll reflect on a few things I'm grateful for in my life. It could be big things ("being safe and healthy") or small things ("Lunch today was yummy" or "I'm glad I had a good conversation with Peter"). Taking one small moment to reflect on what you're grateful for can be a really healthy way to end your night.

- **Go to bed.** Finally, I'll lie down and prepare myself to fall asleep. At this point, my brain is usually all set to turn off, so it doesn't take me too long to pass out (within 10 or 15 minutes). If I find my brain still being a bit active, I may think some more about things I'm grateful for or things that went well during my day.

My nighttime ritual is fairly straightforward, but the point is that it works for me. It helps me to relax and end my day on an overall positive and enjoyable note. Your nighttime ritual may look quite different, depending on your personality, interests, and responsibilities. The goal is to carve out at least some time and space at the end of your day to "do your thing" and unwind a bit. This is important not just for preparing to go to sleep, but also for your overall mental well-being.

Depending on your personal obligations, it may be difficult to find time and space for yourself at the end of the night. But even being able to spend 30 minutes watching a favorite TV show and cuddling with a pet or loved one can be a valuable way to relax and begin to turn off your mind.

How you spend your night is going to vary from day to day. Some days I'd rather put on a podcast or read a book than watch a movie. On weekend nights, especially, I may want to go out to a restaurant, movie, concert, or dance class. Your nighttime ritual isn't some hard and fast schedule that you need to follow exactly every day. It's just a general guideline for how you think it would be best to end most of your days.

 **exercise**

Creating Your Nighttime Ritual

STEP **1.** Revisit your "Daily Routine" exercise from Chapter 1, focusing specifically on your nighttime habits.

STEP **2.** Reflect on the nighttime ritual you're presently following. Ask yourself:

- "Is my current night ritual helping me to get into a relaxed and calm state?"

- "Is my current night ritual ending the day on a positive note?"

- "Is my current night ritual preparing me for sleep, or is it keeping me awake?"

STEP **3.** Now take a piece of paper and pen (or open up a new text document on your computer) and write "Nighttime Ritual" at the top of the page.

STEP **4.** Make a step-by-step list of your ideal nighttime ritual.

- Consider activities that help you to relax, wind down, and enjoy yourself toward the end of your night.

- Consider activities that give your night meaning, such as reflecting on things you're grateful for, writing in a journal, or engaging in some type of meditation/prayer.

- Consider activities that give you a head start on the next day, such as making a short "to do" list for tomorrow.

- Include all basic habits related to hygiene and getting ready for bed—brushing your teeth, washing your face, taking any medication/vitamins, etc.

- Think about whether you can "stack" certain habits—such as repeating affirmations while brushing your teeth.

STEP **5.** Once you've completed your list, reflect on how each step in your nighttime ritual serves the broader perspective in your life. Remember that rituals should be infused with some sense of meaning and purpose.

STEP **6.** Save the document in your self-improvement folder.

Nice—you've completed the exercise!

Nighttime rituals don't have to be complicated, but you should pay careful attention to them, because how you end your day can have a big psychological impact on how you feel about your life. Psychology teaches us that the beginning and ending of an experience often sticks in our minds more than whatever happens in between. The same is true for how we spend our days. If you can learn how to *start* your days on a positive note and *end* your days on a positive note, you will be in a powerful position in your life. Then everything that happens in between can begin to fall into place.

CHAPTER NINE

Systems and Goals: Crafting a New Lifestyle

Goals are a major focus in self-improvement, for obvious reasons. We become interested in changing ourselves so that we can achieve some sort of direct *result* in our lives. However, thinking of self-improvement in terms of goals can be a double-edged sword. For many people, setting goals and deadlines can motivate them and keep them focused; but for others, setting goals may actually be a way to set themselves up for failure.

When we set a goal, we typically make a declaration to ourselves, such as "lose 20 pounds" or "make a six-figure salary." Then we work our butts off to reach our specific goal. We might even set a deadline for ourselves—"before the summer starts" or "by the time I reach 30"—to put extra pressure on ourselves. But there are many ways that this can backfire on us. What if you only lose 10 pounds before summer? You've still made progress, even though you didn't reach your goal. Does that mean you've failed? Does it mean you should give up?

And even when we are lucky enough to achieve our stated goals, it doesn't mean that our work is finished. We must also be able to *sustain* the change into the future. If you lose the 20 pounds, technically your goal has been reached. But if you can't keep up with your changes in diet and exercise and you gain back that 20 pounds, it's almost as if you never succeeded at all. It might even sting more than if you'd failed in the first place.

This is why, according to *How to Fail at Almost Everything and Still Win Big* by Scott Adams, "goals" tend to be short-term thinking, while "systems" tend to be long-term thinking. If you're looking to make a sustainable change or improvement to your life, what you really need to create is a *system* that works for you. Goals can be good temporary motivators, but often they aren't enough for true change.

Creating the right systems in your life can energize and sustain you long into the future. This doesn't mean that goals are necessarily a bad thing, but it's important that you approach them in the right way. This chapter will provide guidelines on how to think more systematically about your life and create a system that actually works for you. You will also learn how to properly set and pursue goals without losing sight of the wider view.

Systems and Long-Term Change

One of the key differences between systems and goals is that *systems* are focused on small but long-term change. Unlike goals, systems don't require a benchmark that we must reach within a certain limited time frame. Instead, they represent a daily approach to life that we continuously practice and gradually build on.

This book is all about how small changes can lead to big changes over time. Almost every piece of advice in this book is a small change that you could start *today* if you really wanted. Small changes aren't instant fixes, but they are sustainable, and their influence can add up over time.

If you focus on small and gradual change, years from now you will look back and barely recognize your former self. This is how most change unfolds in our lives. On a day-by-day basis, it might not feel as if you are changing much. It's only when you look back that you see what a big difference you've made.

Here are some examples of the difference between goals and systems:

- Diet: Losing 20 pounds is a goal but eating right is a system.

- Exercise: Running a marathon in under four hours is a goal but going to the gym daily is a system.

- Writing: Writing a novel is a goal but writing a little each day is a system.

- Business: Making a million dollars is a goal, but creating valuable products and services is a system.

- Relationships: Finding a boyfriend/girlfriend is a goal but being more social on the weekends is a system.

Do you see the difference? Systems are focused on a *process* rather than any specific outcome. Building the right system can help you reach your goals, but your focus is primarily on what you're doing every day. Your system is your everyday habits and routine. Creating a system means building a *lifestyle*, not just trying to reach a specific goal.

You already have a system in place in your life. It's your daily routine. This gives you a picture of the systems currently running in your life. Are they working for you or against you?

Your daily routine is a microcosm of your entire life. The small things you do over and over on a daily basis will eventually build up to what you become in the future. Here's how to think more systematically about your life and your self-improvement.

Growth Mindset vs. Fixed Mindset

One big concept in psychology right now is the "growth mindset." The basic concept is that we have the capacity to change and improve ourselves over time. This is in contrast to a fixed mindset, in which we believe that the way we are now is the way we are always going to be—and there's no hope of changing that.

According to a fascinating study published in *The Journal of Child Psychology and Psychiatry* in 2017, even a single 30-minute lesson about growth mindset can help young teens who have symptoms of depression and anxiety. The study first measured symptoms of anxiety and depression by having individuals take a self-reported survey. (Parents were also asked to take a survey to assess symptoms in their children.) Only individuals who reported severe symptoms of depression were accepted into the study.

Some participants were then assigned to take a 30-minute computer session that taught them about new findings in psychology and the benefits of a growth mindset. This included research showing that our personalities are much more malleable and subject to change than we think they are. It also covered the idea of "neuroplasticity," which explains that our brains are always building new neural connections based on new experiences. The teens were then given examples of how a growth mindset could be applied to their daily lives. Older youths shared their personal experiences about how a growth mindset had helped them deal with problems such as embarrassment and rejection.

Researchers then did follow-ups with each participant after three, six, and nine months in order to assess whether their symptoms of anxiety and depression had changed. The participants who had taken the mini-course on growth mindset reported fewer symptoms of anxiety and depression in all follow-ups. Even a single 30-minute lesson about growth mindset can have a significant long-term impact.

In the context of depression and anxiety (or any mental condition), a growth mindset can be tremendously important, because it at least leaves us open to the *possibility* of change. By being more open to that possibility, we are more likely to try new things and take advantage of opportunities that might help us in some way.

A fixed mindset, on the other hand, will lead you to give up and remain stuck in your old ways. You'll think to yourself, "What's the point of trying new things if I'm always going to be exactly the same?" And that fixed mindset keeps feeding on itself, leaving you trapped in the same patterns. This makes change nearly impossible.

The same study also shows how helpful it can be to learn more about psychology in general. The more we know about how our minds work and the better we understand ourselves, the more we can use that information to improve our lives. Learning about concepts such as growth mindset and neuroplasticity teaches us that we actually have some power over our lives and what type of people we become.

This is a critical lesson for children and teens, who may inhibit their education, growth, and development if they believe there's no hope for changing their ways. After learning about the concept of growth mindset, the young people in the study were more likely to agree with statements such as these:

- "I can be popular with kids my age if I really try."

- "I can do well on tests if I really try hard."

- "I can usually find something good to like, even in a bad situation."

- "When I have a problem that I can't change, I can take my mind off of it."

These are empowering beliefs that can motivate anyone to become a better person and take more control over his or her life. Teaching these attitudes in schools could make a huge difference in the world by encouraging every child to reach for his or her fullest potential.

A growth mindset is just as important in adults. Even when we're older, we continue to learn, grow, and evolve as human beings. Self-improvement is a never-ending process and understanding that is essential for building a consistent growth mindset.

It's amazing how a one-time 30-minute lesson could have such a long-term positive impact. But imagine how much *more* powerful it could be if you reminded yourself every day to maintain a growth mindset. One way to do this is to create affirmations that emphasize growth, progress, and gradual improvement. Consider adding these to your list of affirmations:

- "I'm growing and evolving a little bit each day
- "Every experience is an opportunity to learn and improve."
- "I'm a dynamic person who is changing every day."

Changing your mindset isn't easy, and it doesn't happen overnight. But actively working toward a growth mindset is a shift in perspective that can make a big difference in how you live your life and evolve as a person. The truth is that we're always changing, in ways both small and large. The idea that we have a fixed self is a myth.

In one insightful study published in *Psychology and Aging* in 2016, researchers found that people often underestimate how much their personalities will change over the course of a lifetime. They had participants take a personality test at the age of 14 and then again at 77, and they found that individuals scored quite differently on various mental traits.

This shows us that we may change a lot more than we realize, and our idea of a "self" is much more dynamic than we think. Keep this in mind as you cultivate a growth mindset.

Try this thought experiment.

Think about the kind of person you were 5, 10, or 20 years ago—or back when you were a child. How was that person different from who you are today? You can probably identify at least a few major differences. In the same way, who you will be 5, 10, or 20 years into the future will be different from who you are right now.

We're always changing, but often it's not until we look back at our lives that we realize just how much has changed over time. Understanding this is essential for embracing your dynamic self and cultivating a growth mindset that aims for long-term progress and improvement.

Imagining Your Future Self

Honestly, how often do you think about your future self? Your answer to this question could make a big difference in how happy and successful you will be later in life.

Your future self is an important concept to think about when you're trying to create a life and daily routine that serves your long-term goals. By asking yourself where you want to be in the future, you can make smarter choices in the present.

In the daily hustle and bustle, it's easy to get caught up in the present moment and take a narrow view of how to live our lives. We tend to focus more on our immediate needs and wants than on what we want in the future. We can become addicted to instant gratification. The way we use the internet is one of the best examples of this. We think of something we want to buy, and we order it on Amazon that same day. We think of a video we want to watch, and we search for it on YouTube. We post a random opinion on social media and get instant "likes."

We want things *now* and not later—even if that means rejecting a bigger and better reward in the future. This seems to be truer today than ever before.

Psychologists have observed this in the classic "marshmallow experiment," in which most children are likely to eat a single marshmallow right away rather than wait 10 minutes to get two marshmallows. But studies also show that the children who can resist the immediate reward in order to receive a bigger reward in the future are more likely to be successful in school, work, and life.

In fact, one of the biggest factors in self-improvement and smart decision-making is knowing when to pay short-term costs for long-term benefits. To do this, we need to keep the future in mind at all times and consider our future self. Only considering our needs and wants in the present moment can lead to impulsive decisions that come back to bite you. For example, we want to eat that slice of cake *now* because it will give us pleasure—and that's a nice experience. But if we always give in to such instant rewards, we'll likely end up paying major costs in the future, such as bad health and obesity. This is why it's so important to think and act with a long-term mindset. We need to pay attention to how the things we do *today* are going to influence where we are *tomorrow*.

There has been some interesting psychology research showing how thinking about your future self can improve your life in different ways. In one study published in the *Journal of Consumer Research* in 2011, it was found that individuals who felt more connected to their future self ended up consuming less and saving more out of their paychecks.

This makes perfect sense. If you consider your future wants and needs, you're going to act differently today from how you would act if you completely ignored the future. Want to buy a new car? Want to go on a vacation or save up for college? Want to have backup funds in case of an emergency? All of these things will require that you consume less now so that you can build up to something bigger in the future.

In another study published in *Psychological Science* in 2013, it was found that individuals are more likely to make such future-oriented decisions when they feel more powerful and in control of their lives. Perhaps too many people underestimate the influence they have over their own future, so they begin to neglect it entirely. It's easy to see how our actions influence the present, but it's harder to imagine how our actions will influence us months, years, and decades down the road.

Happy and successful people are strongly connected to their future self. They see where they want to be in 5, 10, and 20 years, and they see how they can start moving in that direction *today*.

Connecting with Your Future Self

By connecting with your future self, you can begin to make changes that put you on a path toward long-term growth and improvement. Try the following exercises to connect more with your future self.

Exercise 1. Take a few minutes and ask yourself, "How are my actions today influencing where I will be in the future?" Look at your daily routine with a long-term mindset. Are your daily habits serving your future goals or not?

Exercise 2. Write a letter from the perspective of your future self, giving advice to your present self. What kind of advice might that future you give to today's you? What insights could you potentially gain? This is a terrific exercise to take you outside of your present mindset and more into the mindset of your potential future self.

Exercise 3. Imagine what your life will look like 5, 10, or 20 years into the future. What are some possible paths that you might travel? What will your daily routine be like? How can you live more like this future self today?

Your aim with these three exercises is to start merging your present self with your future self. You can do this by *acting as if you already are this future self*. In one of the exercises above, you were asked to consider what your daily routine would be like in an ideal future. Now ask yourself how you can begin integrating those habits into your current routine. Start acting as if you are already this future self. By approaching your life this way, you'll begin to make big changes.

Letting Go of Perfectionism

One big obstacle to growth-oriented thinking is the idea of perfectionism: the false belief that we can live our lives without ever making any mistakes or failing at anything. This puts an unrealistic burden on us to think that we must always be "perfect" or we might as well not try to do anything at all.

This perfectionist mindset can hinder our growth and cause us to give up without attempting to change our lives at all. If you believe that you must be perfect in everything you do, then you may not see a point in trying new things, challenging yourself, or trying to improve yourself gradually.

When building new habits into your routine, don't be surprised when you find yourself slipping up and making mistakes. That's natural. And it's all a part of the growth process. It's easy to become frustrated along the path of self-improvement—almost too easy. We try to make a positive change, we slip up and make a mistake, and we quickly think "forget it" and give up.

Consider the example of someone who is trying to quit smoking. They try to quit cold turkey, successfully go a few days without a cigarette, then cave in and smoke one while out socializing one night. We may look back at an experience like this and consider it a total failure. When we cave in even once, we begin to think "what the hell" and just give up. In fact, psychologists are starting to call this the "what the hell" effect.

One study published in *Appetite* in 2010 illustrates this perfectly. Researches found that individuals who were dieting ate more cookies if they had been served a "larger" slice of pizza. In other words, eating that slice of pizza had a "what the hell" effect, so they ended up eating more cookies than dieters who hadn't eat the "large" slice and therefore didn't feel as bad about eating the pizza.

That "what the hell" effect applies to many areas of life—eating, smoking, consuming alcohol, taking drugs, not going to the gym, or any behavior that we are trying to cut back on. A study published in the *Psychology of Addictive Behaviors* in 2013 points out that sometimes addiction is better overcome without taking a strict vow of abstinence. When someone practices total abstinence, they often have a perfectionist mindset in which they can't allow themselves to make a mistake even once. Because of this, they are much more likely to experience the "what the hell" effect when they make their first mistake.

To avoid this "what the hell" effect, it's important to recognize that self-improvement isn't a linear process, but a jagged and dynamic path. Sometimes you take two steps forward, one step back, one step forward, two steps back, two steps forward, and so it continues. But you can't let any single mistake distract you from the progress that you are making. Two steps forward, one step backwards is still moving forward.

Sure, maybe you gave in and smoked a cigarette, but you also went three days without one. That has to count for something—and you have to start somewhere. Don't let yourself spiral out of control because of one small mistake. Failure can actually be a good sign. It means you are challenging yourself and pushing your limits. Don't necessarily view it as a bad thing, but as an unavoidable part of growing and improving.

If you find yourself getting stuck in a perfectionist mindset, consider adding these to your collection of affirmations:

- "Failure is often the first step to success."

- "No single event in the past defines me. Keep moving forward."

- "The bigger picture is more important than any single detail."

- "A small step forward is still a step forward."

These are good beliefs to instill within yourself. Use them as tools to help shift your perspective toward more systematic and growth-oriented thinking.

Thinking Systematically

We've focused on the big ideas behind systematic and growth-oriented thinking. There's no simple, magic solution to change your mindset, but these are important principles to keep in mind as you try to improve your daily life.

Here's a recap of the core principles to keep in mind when trying to think more systematically about your life.

Your daily habits determine your future. Make sure to think about the long-term consequences of your daily actions.

Apply a growth mindset. Always remember that you have the ability to change over time. You are not a "fixed self" that will always be the same exact person you are today. It may be a slow process, but growth is possible.

Keep your future self in mind. While it's important to focus on how you can change in the present, there's also tremendous power in projecting your future self to have a clear idea of where you want to go in your life. This can play a major role in how you act now.

Accept failures. There is no process of growth and improvement that doesn't include experiencing failure along the way. Think of your mistakes as short-term bumps on your road to long-term improvement.

Do what works for you. Happy and successful people don't all follow the same routine; they devise a system that caters to their individual preferences, values, and needs. Don't feel the need to copy anyone else.

Be patient with yourself. The biggest trap in all of self-improvement is to think that you can change yourself and your life overnight. We crave quick solutions, but growth can be a slow process. It's essential that we learn to be patient with ourselves.

The major difference between "systematic thinking" and "goals thinking" is that with systematic thinking you hold a long-term view of the future and what you are trying to build toward each day. It's not just about pushing yourself for a few months to reach a particular goal but building a *lifestyle* that you can sustain endlessly.

One mantra I live by is to "think big, act small." While most of the recommendations in this book are about making small changes, you must also keep the broader view in mind. That's why systematic thinking is essential.

Try to think of your complete daily routine as a system in itself. Each daily habit is a small component that helps the system to run efficiently. Is this system working for you or working against you?

Small Steps: Work

- Make a list of things you like about your current job

- Always get to work on time

- Make a daily "to do" list

- Do the most important, difficult, and urgent tasks first

- Break big goals into smaller tasks

- Know when to ask for help

- Continue gaining knowledge and learning new skills

- Go to work parties to strengthen your relationships with coworkers

- Schedule small breaks to recharge

- Reward yourself when you do an awesome job

- Play music to keep you motivated while you work (if appropriate in your workplace)

- Be happy for other people's success and learn from them

- Don't wait until the last minute to meet a deadline

- Have fun by starting a healthy competition with coworkers

- Be as friendly as possible toward everyone you work with

- Help your coworkers when they ask for it—be a team player

- Don't be afraid to say "no" if you're genuinely busy

- Bring positive energy to work—smile more, laugh more, be optimistic

- Make your internet homepage something productivity-related, such as emails

- Ask your boss what he or she needs from you—be extra helpful

- Be open to feedback from others (coworkers, your boss), and don't take it personally

- Don't be afraid to share your opinions—in a polite way, of course

- Encourage everyone to be their best self.

- Reflect on the bigger picture behind your work.

Goals and Short-Term Motivation

While creating systems is the most effective method for self-improvement in the long term, setting goals can still be a valuable way to motivate yourself and push yourself forward.

A goal is any objective that someone wants to achieve. The basic structure behind every goal is "Present State ⟶ Desired Future State." Your present state is where you are right now, and your desired future state is where you want to be after you accomplish your goal. A common goal might be to lose 10 pounds. Your current weight would be your present state, and that weight minus 10 pounds is your desired future state.

Every goal can be conceptualized into these two stages in some way. Trying to achieve our goals is always a process of moving from one state in life to another. This applies to all types of goals, whether they are related to health, career, relationships, education, sports, hobbies, or just happiness in general.

How to Set Goals

Before trying to achieve any goal, it's important to know how to set the goal properly in the first place. The criteria for setting goals are summarized in the acronym SMART, popularized by psychologist and organizational expert Peter Drucker. According to this model, the best way to set a goal is to make your goal:

Specific. One major problem is that people make their goals too vague and abstract. They say their goal is to "be happy," "be healthy," or "be nicer," but they don't tie that to a specific outcome. Be as concrete as possible so that you know exactly what you want to accomplish. Instead of setting a goal to "be healthy," set a goal that "I will go to the gym five times a week" or "I will beat my last time for the local 10K race."

Measurable. Your goal should be specific but also measurable so that you can track your progress. Try to set your goal in terms of a number, such as "I will lose X pounds," "I will go the gym X times per week," or "I will write X words each day." By assigning a number to reach, you can more easily measure your success. Keep track in a daily journal or with a mobile app so that you can visually see the progress you are making, which will help to keep you motivated and committed.

Achievable. Be sure that your goal is actually achievable. You wouldn't want to set a goal of benching 300 pounds after going to the gym for one month; a number that's slightly above your current best is more within your grasp. By setting goals that are challenging but still reachable, you can push yourself forward without setting yourself up for failure and disappointment.

Relevant. Your goal should be relevant to your core values and where you want to go in the future. There's no point in setting goals just to prove to yourself that you can achieve them. Aim toward goals that serve the bigger picture behind your life. If you value your health, then set goals to help you become healthier. If you value your work, set goals to help you become more productive. If you value your family, set goals to help you build stronger relationships. Don't just set goals for the sake of doing so. Make sure they are tied to a core value in your life and a clear vision of the future you want to build for yourself.

Time-Bound. Set a deadline to shoot for, telling yourself that you have to achieve your goal within a certain time frame. Deadlines can be an important aspect of goal-setting, because they give you something specific to aim for. They can motivate you to work harder and faster to achieve your goal by the deadline you've set for yourself.

Every goal you set should follow these five principles. It should be specific, measurable, achievable, relevant, and time-bound. Without these elements we can set ourselves up for failure. Combining these criteria with the other information in this book (especially your "Tools for Motivation" in Chapter 6) will put you in a great position to be successful. That doesn't mean you will achieve every goal you set. That's when your systematic thinking needs to kick back in. Understand that no single failure is final and that multiple failures often are necessary along any path to success.

Creating a Progressive Timeline of Goals

At the beginning of this book, I asked you to create a detailed list of your daily routine. This was fundamental to the core lessons in this book, because it focused your attention on the small habit changes you can start working on every day. In this section, I'm introducing an exercise that directly connects your daily routine to your bigger goals in life. I call this a "Progressive Timeline of Your Goals" because it begins by focusing on goals to complete within a single day, then expands to goals you aim to complete within a week, a month, a year, and a decade.

By creating a progressive timeline of goals, you begin to get a more complete picture of where you want to go in life. This includes zooming in on goals you can accomplish today and zooming out on goals you want to achieve far into the future.

Writing down your goals is a good way to make your dreams become more tangible. It doesn't replace actually taking action to achieve those goals, but being able to see them written out in front of you is a first step toward being more proactive. To give you an idea of what this might look like, here's an example of my own progressive timeline.

My Goals Timeline

Within a Day

- Answer today's work emails.

- Finish writing this chapter.

- Go grocery shopping.

- Call parents to check up on them.

- Go to the gym.

Within a Week

- Record a new podcast.

- Write a new article for my website.

- Get new clothes for summer.

- Do maintenance check on car.

- Pay my bills for the month.

- Do something fun with friends on the weekend.

Within a Month

- Start recording for new music project.

- Find new coaching clients.

- Go to a concert.

- Brainstorm on ways to promote new book.

- Keep making articles and podcasts.

Within a Year

- Take a vacation and visit back home.

- Start writing next book.

- Finish recording music album.

- Start dating seriously again.

- Take active steps to expand my network and social circle.

- Find new ways to promote website and brand.

Within 5 Years

- Move out of apartment and find better home.

- Travel around the world.

- Start writing a screenplay.

- Finish writing next book.

- Write a stand-up comedy routine and try it out.

- Start a self-improvement workshop.

Within 10 Years

- Get married and start a family.

- Finish screenplay and get a movie deal.

- Start a new business with friends in an area I really care about.

- Become more involved in volunteering and social activism.

- Start investing money in other projects and organizations I care about.

Now create a progressive timeline of your own. Focus on what you want to do within the next day ⟶ week ⟶ month ⟶ year ⟶ 5 years ⟶ 10 years. I recommend at least five items for each point on your timeline. This should give you enough flexibility to touch on various aspects of your life that you want to improve. Once you've finished your timeline, save it in your self-improvement folder.

This exercise allows you both to zoom in on short-term goals (within the coming day, week, and month) and zoom out on long-term goals (within the next year, five years, and decade). Once you've created your timeline, you can go back and change it whenever you want. In a month, you may realize you've forgotten a key goal. In a year, you may change your mind about pursuing a past goal. It's all subject to change. The purpose of this exercise is to give you a clearer idea of both your short-term goals and your long-term goals, and how they may fit together. But there's nothing wrong with abandoning certain goals and ambitions as you move through life, especially as your own values and preferences change. So, don't worry about making your timeline perfect.

This is a useful exercise to revisit at least once per year. It's a good reminder of your long-term goals and ambitions, and it gives you a rough time frame for when you expect to fulfill these goals. Several years down the road, it will be interesting to look back on your timeline to see how far you've come toward achieving certain goals and how your interest in other goals may have changed.

Conclusion:
Big Perspective, Tiny Changes

Although lots of tips and suggestions have been offered throughout this book, it's important to remember the fundamental idea: *start small and focus on making tiny changes.*

It's easy to become overwhelmed by all the choices we have in life, but the best path forward is to focus on one small habit change and build from there. Self-improvement takes time, effort, and patience. It's not something that happens overnight, and there are no quick solutions that will magically make things better.

I've been practicing this advice for more than a decade now, but I still have a lot of learning to do. I'm still imperfect. I still have flaws. I still make mistakes on a daily basis. But, I'm making progress.

Change *is* possible.

I sincerely hope that the ideas in these pages have already helped you in some small way. Choosing to adopt any one of the small habits suggested in these pages can make a big difference over the long term.

Please use this book as a resource to learn from, return to, and integrate into your life. Share it with family members and friends you think would benefit from its message. And most importantly, keep growing and improving yourself.

—Steven Handel

Appendix:
Collection of Small Habits

Throughout this book there are many suggestions on small habits you can begin integrating into your daily routine. Here is a comprehensive collection of most of the small habits recommended (as well as other small habits that weren't mentioned).

Think of this collection of small habits as the nuts and bolts you can use to build up your daily routine. They are the tiniest of actions you can do on a daily basis that promote happiness, growth, and well-being.

Though it would be impossible to do all of these tasks in a single day, there are likely a couple good suggestions in each section that you could begin integrating into your life as soon as possible.

This is a good resource to go back to when evaluating your daily routine and trying to find new things to add to it. Though a lot of these habits are common sense, it's helpful to be reminded of the little things that can often make a big difference in our lives.

Sleep

Keep a regular sleep schedule. A consistent sleep schedule is key to balancing your body's energy levels (the times of the day you feel awake vs. when you feel sleepy).

Aim for 7 to 10 hours of sleep each night. Most health professionals recommend 7 to 10 hours for the average person (but there can be exceptions depending on the individual).

Set an alarm for going to bed as well as waking up. Alarms help you keep your schedule on track. Set an alarm for when you wake up, but also for when you should begin winding down and getting ready for sleep.

Be physically active during the day so that you'll be tired at night. Physical activity burns off energy, stress, and anxiety, which will make it easier to fall asleep at night.

Use your bedroom for sleeping, not for TV/computer. Try to make your bedroom a place that is dedicated to sleep and not other activities. This will build a strong association in your brain so that by the time your head hits the pillow your body is thinking, "Oh, it's sleep time."

Make sure your pillows and sheets are clean and comfortable. Feeling comfortable and clean will make it easier for your body to fall asleep peacefully. Try to wash or change your sheets at least once per week.

Brush your teeth and wash your face before you go to bed. This is a nice activity to do right before you go to bed so that you feel clean and refreshed.

Dim the lights an hour before sleep time. Bright lights keep us energized while darker rooms put us into a more relaxed and sleepy state. Try dimming the lights or lighting candles at night to signal to your body that it's time to slow down.

Stop using electronics 30 minutes before bedtime. This is another good way to begin winding down and preparing your body for sleep. Too much TV, social media, or video games (especially late at night) will keep your mind overstimulated.

Eat a light snack but no big meals before bed. Too much food before you go to sleep can lead to indigestion, heartburn, or nausea. If you need to have something to eat, make sure it's a light snack.

Read a book, meditate, take a bath, or do something relaxing. Find activities to do at night that put your body into a relaxed state and help you to wind down at the end of the day.

Open a window to let in fresh air while you sleep. Fresh air will improve the quality of your sleep, so it's a good idea to crack a window open and have good ventilation in your bedroom.

Close the blinds, turn off any lights, and make the room as dark as possible. Our brains naturally associate darkness with rest, so turn off any lights that aren't necessary.

Play soothing sounds to help you fall asleep. Many people find that playing soothing sounds (like waterfalls, rain, waves, or ambient music) helps them to fall asleep more quickly. You can find free apps or playlists on your computer or phone for this.

Visualize yourself in a relaxing place. If you have trouble relaxing, or your mind is too busy, practice visualizing yourself at a calm place, such as at the beach on a summer day, staring at the stars at night, or in a room filled with soft pillows.

Practice slow, deep breathing to calm your body and mind. Slow breathing is a known way to calm your body and mind. Practice slowly inhaling through your nose, taking a quick one-second pause, then slowly exhaling through your mouth. (You can also do this in combination with listening to soothing sounds or visualizing yourself in a relaxing place).

Place a glass of water by your bed. Just in case you get thirsty at night, it's better to have a glass of water next to you rather than having to get out of bed and walk to the other room to get a drink (which will wake you up a lot more).

Cuddle with a loved one, a pet, or even a stuffed animal. Often, being able to cuddle with someone (or something) can have a calm, soothing effect on us, which makes it easier to fall asleep.

If you can't sleep, get up and do something for 15 minutes. If you're laying in bed for a while and you can't fall asleep, get up and do an easy, repetitive task for a bit. Wash the dishes, fold laundry, or clean something. It will burn off extra energy and put you in a tired state.

Diet

Drink water at every meal. Water is one of our most basic needs and it's a lot healthier than drinking soda or sugary drinks.

Eat vegetables and greens with every meal. Vegetables are an important part of our daily nutrition.

Cut down on sugar, fast food, and junk food (such as salty snacks). Sugar and salt can be the most harmful parts of our diet if we overconsume them.

Eat less red meat. Try to limit yourself to just one meal with red meat per week. Focus more on chicken, fish, or other non-beef alternatives.

Plan and prepare your meals out before the week starts. When you plan and prepare your meals ahead of time, it'll make you less likely to go for convenient options (like fast food).

Eat an early breakfast to get your metabolism going. An early breakfast, even if it's just a small one like a banana and cup of coffee, can help wake up your body and get your metabolism going.

Cook your own meals instead of eating out. When we cook our own meals, we are more aware of what we are consuming than when we eat food that is prepared for us.

Serve yourself smaller portions. When we put food on our plates, we're motivated to finish everything, even when we are already full.

Eat slowly and mindfully—and notice when you are full. Many people eat too fast and that leads them to eat more than is necessary. Practice eating more slowly. Savor each bite and be more mindful of the taste, smell, and texture.

Avoid snacking while you're distracted or watching TV. When you're watching a TV show or movie, it's easy to mindlessly snack on junk food without paying attention to how much you're consuming.

Diet with a friend so that you can hold each other accountable. Dieting with a friend gives you an extra boost in motivation because you are both working toward a common goal and can make sure you are staying on track together.

Pay attention to how your body responds to different foods. Often when you eat something unhealthy your body responds to it in a negative way; you may feel nauseous or fatigued. Paying attention to how your body responds to different foods will help you to make smarter choices.

Check the nutrition label of everything you eat. We often don't realize what is in the food we eat, so it's always helpful to check the nutrition label. Pay attention to servings, calories, sugar, salt, and fats.

Avoid emotional eating—eat to nourish, not to cope. People fall into the habit of eating when they are bored or in a bad mood, but we should approach eating with the intent to nourish ourselves, not to cope with our problems.

Surround yourself with healthy snacks, at home and at work. We eat what's readily available to us. If you stock up your home or office with unhealthy snacks, then you're probably going to eat them.

Surround yourself with people who have healthy habits. The people in our lives have a big influence on us, so if you surround yourself with people who eat healthy and stay fit then you'll be more likely to adopt those same habits.

Take a multivitamin daily. While it's best to get all of your nutrients through food, taking a multivitamin can be a good way to make sure you're getting all your daily nutrition needs.

Curb your appetite by drinking coffee or tea. If you're trying to eat less and lose weight, consider substituting your usual snack with a cup of coffee or tea.

Try intermittent fasting on weekends or "off days." Intermittent fasting can be a good way to lose weight and boost your health. If your doctor approves, spend a whole day (or half day) without eating anything (except water, tea, or coffee).

Make fruit/vegetable smoothies to help meet your nutritional needs. If you want an easy way to meet your fruit and vegetable needs, consider throwing some into a blender and creating a smoothie.

Been good all day? Reward yourself with a dessert or "unhealthy snack." It's fine to eat unhealthy food every now and then, but the key is to treat them as a reward and not a daily occurrence.

Exercise

Get out and walk each day. Many people spend too much time indoors, sitting down, and being physically inactive. The simple act of getting outside more and taking a short walk is a great first step in being more physically active.

Stretch to start your morning. At the beginning of the day, take a quick 10 to 15 minutes to stretch your body. Wake yourself and get the blood flowing through your muscles and joints before you jump into your day.

Do push-ups/jumping jacks/sit-ups before you take a shower. These are easy exercises that anyone can do in the morning because they don't require any equipment. Take 10 to 15 minutes to work up a quick sweat before you jump into the shower.

Avoid sitting too much—stand up frequently, even if it's only for a few minutes. If you sit a lot at home or work, it's important that you find opportunities to stand up more, even if it's only for a few minutes. Set an alert on your phone each hour to remind you to get up and take a quick walk around the office or do something while standing.

Do physical activities you find fun (bike riding, swimming, tennis). Instead of running on a treadmill, it might be more exciting for you to get physical doing something you enjoy.

Do a rep of push-ups or sit-ups before you eat a snack. This is a nice way to keep yourself physically active throughout your day in small ways.

Do a rep of pull-ups every time you enter your bedroom or office. Put a pull-up bar in your doorway as a reminder to do a rep of pull-ups every time you enter that room.

Join a sports league with friends. Find a sports league in your local community. This is a fantastic way to keep yourself committed to a fun physical activity.

Go to the gym with someone who will hold you accountable. If you have trouble going to the gym regularly, consider inviting a friend to join you. You can schedule to go at the same time to keep each other on track.

Hang out with fit people. We pick up the habits of the people we spend the most time with, so surrounding yourself with fit and healthy people is going to motivate you to develop those same healthy habits.

Listen to music while you work out. Upbeat music will make your workouts more fun and exciting.

When you can, walk or bike instead of driving. If you plan on going somewhere that is in walking distance or biking distance, consider doing that instead of driving (saves on gas too!).

Practice mind-body exercises, such as yoga or tai chi, to improve body awareness. A big component to your health is becoming more aware of your body and how it works. Yoga, tai chi, and mindful stretching are great ways to do this. Just 10 to 15 minutes each morning is all you need!

Do sports or other physical activities with your kids. Playing sports with your kids, even if it's something as simple as throwing a baseball or playing basketball, is a great way to build a culture of fitness in your family.

Play with your pets—take them on walks, bring them outside, play "wrestle." Taking your dog on a walk every day, or lengthening your usual walk, is a nice way of getting a bit of exercise.

Park farther away so you have to take a mini-walk to get where you want to go. One simple way to get extra physical activity is to park at the opposite end of the parking lot from your destination.

Spend time in nature, even if it's only at a local park. Being around nature can benefit both your physical health and mental health. Find nearby parks, bring a friend along, and go on a short walk or hike.

Make love with your partner more. Making love is a fun and enjoyable way to be physically active and connect with your partner more on an intimate level—a great form of exercise!

Cleaning

Make your bed every morning. It feels good to complete a task and build momentum, plus you get to come back home to a clean bed.

Minimize your possessions. Most people own so much stuff that they don't know what to do with it or where to put it. Keep things simple and stick to the essentials.

To let go of a sentimental object, take a picture of it. If you're finding it difficult to part with an item that you don't need, take a picture of it to save the memory. If you think some items you don't need still have value, consider donating them to a charity or giving them to a friend.

Don't leave a room without cleaning up first. A great habit to have is to clean your messes as soon as you make them. For example, don't let dirty plates sit and pile up, just wash them right after you finish eating.

Throw dirty clothes directly into the laundry bin. Laundry can pile up and get out of hand if we don't take care of it right away.

Split cleaning duties if you live with others. Everyone in the household should pitch in to do their fair share to keep the home clean and neat. Assign duties for each person and rotate on a weekly basis.

Listen to music to make cleaning more fun. Music always makes tedious and boring tasks more fun and interesting.

Open your windows to let in fresh air. Whenever you can, let fresh air into your home and make sure things don't get stale.

Use flowers and plants to fill your home with nice scents. Flowers and plants also provide fresh oxygen and have a positive psychological effect.

Always clean up after yourself when you're a guest in someone else's home. Do the courtesy of cleaning up after yourself and treating your host's home at least as well as you treat your own.

Remove your shoes indoors. This is just a good way to avoid dragging dirt through your home.

Keep a filing cabinet for important papers. This way, paperwork such as tax documents, contracts, etc., will be organized in one place. Be sure to set up an organizational system that you can follow, and keep it up.

Launder your bed sheets weekly. Make sure your sheets are always clean and smelling fresh. This will also help you sleep better.

Put things away as soon as you finish using them. It only takes a bit of effort, but saves a lot of time and stress in the long run.

Dedicate a chunk of time each week to cleaning. Choose a specific day and time each week to schedule one to two hours of solid cleaning: vacuuming, dusting, scrubbing bathrooms, etc.

Once a year, devote a day to a "tidying marathon." Dedicate one day a year to a thorough "tidying marathon." This is when you go through your entire home cleaning everything and throwing out any junk you no longer need. Doing this will make it easier to maintain a neat and tidy home for the rest of the year.

Money

Save at least 10 percent of every paycheck. Savings are important for big expenses, especially emergencies, luxury expenses, or vacations.

Budget for your monthly needs. Take the time to figure out what your monthly budget is. How much do you typically need per month to pay for food, rent, bills, and other expenses?

Shop at thrift stores and garage sales. These are great places to find cheap clothes, appliances, and other things that you normally would pay a lot more for at a retail store.

Make food at home instead of eating out. Making food on your own can be far cheaper than eating in restaurants.

Don't buy stuff just to signal affluence or status. Instead of trying to "keep up with the Joneses," just focus on your personal needs and wants.

Consider choosing a job that offers upward mobility. If you're searching for a new job or career, consider how much room there is for growth and upward mobility.

Start a side project to make some extra income. Selling clothes or arts and crafts that you make, or writing a blog are a couple of the ways you can channel your passions into extra money.

Be mindful of credit card use, and don't let debt grow. It's all too easy to buy things we can't afford, especially if we just charge it on our credit card. Be very cautious about how you build up debt, and make sure you have a plan to pay it off as soon as possible.

Find cheap or free things to do on the weekends. We don't need to spend much money to find fun things to do in our free time. Most communities plan local events, concerts, and festivals that are cheap or free to attend. You can also visit your local park, library, bowling alley, or mini-golf course. Find event calendars in your area and follow what's going on each week that's fun and cheap.

Hold a garage sale to sell things you don't need. If you have a lot of stuff lying around that you think is valuable but you don't need, consider selling your castoffs at a garage sale or through online resellers like eBay or Amazon.

Keep the future in mind—don't just consume for the present. Studies show that keeping your "future self" in mind can curb impulsive spending and consumerism. When making a big purchase, ask yourself "Is this something I'm still going to value years later?"

Learn how to fix your own furniture and appliances. It's smart to learn how to make basic repairs around the house (especially broken appliances), so that you don't always need to hire someone to do it for you.

Use hand-me-downs from family and friends. Consider reaching out to family and friends and find out if they have any clothes, appliances, or other items that they no longer need. (This is especially useful for supplies for babies and kids).

Take good care of your belongings so they'll last longer. Be gentle with your possessions and perform regular maintenance when needed, and you'll save money by keeping big-ticket items longer, such as your cars, computers, major appliances, etc.

Learn to cut your own hair. You'll save a lot if this is something you can do on your own rather than hire a professional to do it for you.

Focus on buying experiences, not stuff. Studies show that people often get more happiness and life satisfaction when they focus on experiences rather than stuff. Are you building memories with your purchases or just accumulating things?

Buy a car that's reliable and economical. Cars and gas money are often some of the biggest expenses we have, so finding a car that is economical can save you a lot of money in the long-term.

Store and reuse leftover food. Don't waste good food. Get yourself some nice containers to store leftovers and make it a point to eat your leftovers within the next couple days so they don't go bad.

Take advantage of discounts or sales, but only for things you're already planning to buy. Focus on purchases that you were *already* planning to make, and not just buying something because, "Wow, it's 25 percent off!"

Always carry some extra money hidden away in your wallet. Keep extra money tucked away that you will only touch in case of emergency.

Don't gamble money you're not willing to lose. The Number One rule if you're going to gamble or make a risky investment is to be prepared to lose it all. Imagine the worst-case scenario; would you still come out fine?

Keep back-up money somewhere in your house to use for emergencies. This is just in case there is a blackout or some other emergency where you can't access a bank or ATM.

Remember that money is just a tool, it's up to you how to use it. Never forget that money isn't necessarily a "good" or "bad" thing, it's just a tool and it's up to you what you do with it.

Relationships

Say "Hi" to others when you cross paths. Making eye contact with someone or saying "Hi" or "How are you?" shows you're friendly and interested, and others will reciprocate.

Say "please" and "thank you" (even for small things). This basic sign of good manners can go a long way and it shows you are a kind and considerate person.

Be a good listener, giving people time to speak without interruption. Good conversation is just as much about listening as it is about speaking.

Smile more frequently. Smiling makes you look more friendly and attractive.

Treat everyone with respect, regardless of social status. The best sign of good character is that you treat everyone with an equal amount of respect regardless of their position in life.

Make sure that less outgoing people feel included and heard. In many social situations there may be a shy and reserved person who accidentally gets left out of the conversation. Make an attempt to include this person in the conversation.

Be aware of your tone of voice. How you say something is just as important as what you say. Watch your tone of voice and be aware of what messages you're sending to people.

Call your parents once a week, if possible. Stay in touch frequently and show that you care.

Don't talk too loudly in public places. It's common courtesy to respect public places and not disrupt other people.

Put away your phone when talking to people. There's no need to check your texts, emails, or social media while you are face-to-face with someone else.

Show up on time. Always try to get to a scheduled event on time or a bit early. Keeping others waiting for you is often seen as rude and disrespectful.

Treat professional servers with respect. Many people mistreat waiters/waitresses and other professional servers. You can tell a lot about a person by how they treat servers.

Don't talk behind people's backs. Gossiping is unattractive to most people and it can often come back to bite you if you end up spreading lies or things that you shouldn't be sharing.

Avoid nitpicking over other people's mistakes. No one is perfect. There is no need to correct every single mistake a person makes.

Minimize discussion on heated topics. Many times it is best to avoid controversial topics like politics, religion, and philosophy.

Apologize and admit when you're wrong. It's always better to admit when you did something wrong and give a genuine apology than to brush it off or pretend it didn't happen.

Stay in touch with old friends and family, even if it's just with a text. A quick text message saying, "Hi, how are you doing? Hope everything is well!" is all you need to let people know you are keeping them in mind.

Be honest about your thoughts and feelings without being aggressive. It's healthy to be honest and open about how you think and feel, but we must learn to speak our views in a careful way that doesn't come off hostile.

Learn to let others have the last word. It's a good habit to let people get the final word in sometimes and not always feel the need to have a response to everything.

Respect your elders, listen to them and learn from their stories. People who have lived longer than we have often have advice, wisdom, and stories that we can all benefit and learn from.

Write out a personal letter to show someone you care. Writing a personal letter has more of a human touch to it than just sending an email or text message.

Introduce people to each other. One of the best ways to strengthen your social circle is to introduce people to each other and help people build connections. This is a great idea if you have two friends who share similar interests and goals.

If you have criticism for someone, express it to them in private. Criticizing people in public often makes people defensive (and it embarrasses them).

Try to see things from the other person's perspective before passing judgment. Taking time to see things from another person's point-of-view is essential to understanding where they are coming from and learning how to communicate better with them.

Don't make jokes at someone else's expense. There are many ways to be funny without having to bully people, poke fun at their flaws, or make them feel uncomfortable.

Give firm handshakes when meeting new people. A handshake is a big part of the first impression you make on someone.

Forgive and let go when others hurt or disappoint you. Holding onto grudges and disappointments can often hurt your mental health and make it more difficult to improve your relationships.

Give people space when they need it. The best thing you can do in certain situations is give someone time and space to figure things out on their own. Don't become too needy or attached; assume that people will come back to you when they are ready.

Make eye contact with people when speaking with them. Eye contact (but not staring) is an important way we show people that we are listening to them and paying attention.

Be open to feedback from others without taking it personally. A confident person is able to take feedback and criticism from others without overreacting or taking it too seriously.

Reflect on the positive experiences you've enjoyed with people. A great way to strengthen your relationships is to reflect together on the positive experiences you've shared.

Mental Health

Make time in your day for relaxation. Giving yourself time and space to relax is one of the most important ways to combat stress and anxiety.

Spend time around positive people. Studies show that our emotions can be contagious, so try to spend time with people who uplift you and don't bring you down.

Do something creative for 30 minutes each day. Finding a creative hobby that resonates with you can be a great way to express your thoughts and feelings, and improve your general mental health and well-being.

Write about past mistakes and failures to learn from them. Take 10 to 15 minutes to write about a failure that is bothering you and what lessons you can take away from it, and you'll find it easier to let it go.

Write about your individual strengths and past accomplishments. Take 10 to 15 minutes to make a list of your strengths and past accomplishments, then save them somewhere to go back to when you need an extra boost in motivation.

Listen to music to change your mood. Music is one of the most powerful ways we can change our mood and emotions. Create playlists for different moods (uplifting, motivating, relaxing, etc.), and then listen to them when you want to re-create that mood.

Repeat three positive affirmations or quotes every morning. Thinking positively doesn't always come easy, so sometimes we have to practice it.

Minimize your exposure to negative information. News headlines, websites, and social media often focus on negative information because it's more likely to grab your attention. Try to minimize your exposure to this negativity by creating your own positive newsfeeds and knowing when to ignore/block negative people.

Focus on what's in your power to change. One of the biggest contributors to happiness is focusing on what you have the most power to change in your life and ignoring the things that are outside of your influence. Make a list of three things in your life that you have the power to change.

Take a nature walk once a week. Studies show that being around nature can be a huge boost to our mental health and well-being.

Practice mindfulness meditation once a week. Meditation is a highly recommended exercise to boost your happiness and well-being, as well as decrease your stress and anxiety. Find a simple 10- to 15-minute breathing meditation and aim to practice it at least once every week.

Make a list of the things for which you are grateful. Studies show that counting your blessings plays an important role in your mental health. Make a list of 5 to 10 things you are grateful for in your life, then post it somewhere that you'll see it (on your fridge, in your car, above your bed, etc.).

Read two books each year that expand your perspective. Reading books allows us to learn and experience new things that we never get a chance to in the real world.

Do one kind deed each day—with no expectation of receiving anything in return. Doing random acts of kindness can provide another strong boost to our mental health, even if it's something simple like helping someone with homework, giving a compliment, or holding the door for someone.

Find ways to give to your community. It feels good to participate in your community and try to give back as much as possible, especially to the less fortunate. Find local charities or volunteer organizations and find out how you can help.

Spend more time kissing, hugging, and cuddling with loved ones. We all need human affection to feel connected to others.

Take a "mental health" day when you really need it. Sometimes life gets too overwhelming and we just need to take a day to relax and unwind.

Make a list of your core values in life. Focusing on what you truly value in life helps us understand where our priorities should be. Take 10 to 15 minutes and write a list of the core values in your life ("Family," "Work," "Health," etc.) and how you can pursue them better.

Find 10 minutes each day to smile, sing, or dance. It's good to give ourselves the opportunity to express ourselves positively and uplift our spirits.

Write down your negative beliefs on paper, then burn it. This is one little trick to make your negative beliefs less powerful.

Try to find the humor in things, and laugh more. One key to mental health is being able to find the humor in almost anything, especially if you are able to turn around a bad or unpleasant experience and find a way to laugh about it. Laughter itself is a great way to reduce stress and boost positive emotions.

If it's part of your belief system, pray once a day. Prayer can be a great boost to your mental health if you follow a religion or spiritual tradition.

Work

Consider types of work that you enjoy doing. Many of us spend a large chunk of our lives working at a job, so it's important that we pursue a job that we enjoy doing and resonates with us in some way.

Make a list of things you enjoy about your job. Although none of us has the "perfect job," we can still focus on things we enjoy about it (even if it's just liking the people you work with, or feeling a sense of satisfaction when you complete a task).

Always get to work on time. This is one of those small habits that can make you stand out as a responsible employee.

Make a daily "to do" list. Take a moment before you start each day to write down three to five key things that you need to do that day. This will keep you on track, plus it feels good when you get to check things off your list as you complete them.

Do the most important, difficult, and urgent tasks first. Often, we have more energy early in the day rather than later in the day, so many recommend doing the most difficult and urgent tasks first to get them out of the way.

Break big goals into smaller tasks. Any big goal can be broken down into multiple smaller tasks. Focus on what you can do *today* to bring you closer to your goal and continue building from there.

Know when to ask for help. No one can do everything on their own. The most happy and successful people know when it's time to ask for help and guidance.

Continue gaining knowledge and learning new skills. Reading books, watching videos, attending courses, and reaching out to experts are all fantastic ways of building on your knowledge and skills.

Network with people who can help. For many careers, networking with like-minded people is important for success and being able to advance yourself. Make it a point to attend any parties, meetups, or organizations that help you connect with new people.

Schedule small breaks to recharge. Relaxation is just as important as motivation when it comes to being successful.

Reward yourself when you do an awesome job. When you achieve something great at work, feel free to celebrate yourself in small ways such as taking a day off, checking out a new restaurant, or going on a weekend vacation.

Play music to keep you motivated while you work. If appropriate, being able to play music while you work can be a great way to make your day more enjoyable and motivate you to work harder.

Be happy for other people's success, and learn from them. Instead of being jealous of other people's success, be happy for them, congratulate them, and ask them questions to find out what made them so successful.

Don't wait until the last minute to meet a deadline. We often underestimate how long it takes to complete a project (this is known as the "planning fallacy"), so it's important to start your work as soon as possible and get the ball rolling.

Have fun by starting a healthy competition with coworkers. If possible, it can be motivating to set up a friendly competition with the people you work with (such as who can make the most sales in a day, or who can complete their project fastest).

Be as friendly as possible toward all of your coworkers. You have to be with the people you work with on a daily basis, so it'll make things far easier for you if you try to maintain good relationships.

Don't be afraid to say "no" if you're genuinely busy. People have trouble telling others "no" to something because they don't want to disappoint, but if you're too busy it's better to say "no" than to bite off more than you can chew and break your promise.

Make your internet homepage something productivity-related, such as e-mails. This is a good way to remind yourself of work and not get distracted by opening up your social media or emails.

Ask your boss what he or she needs from you—be extra helpful. Every now and then, take a moment to ask your boss, "What do you need from me? What can I be doing better?"

Be open to feedback from others (coworkers, your boss), and don't take it personally. Even if it's not said in the most polite way you can often learn from constructive criticism.

Don't be afraid to share your opinions—in a polite and respectful way. A healthy workplace requires that people are honest and open about how they feel, especially when it comes to how to make things better. Practice being able to speak your mind in a constructive way.

Give compliments to others when they do a good job. People often respond better to positive encouragement than negative comments, so if you see someone improving themselves and doing a good job, then make sure you take the time to point it out and compliment them.

Reflect on the bigger picture behind your work. Every job or career serves a function in society and gives people value in some ways. Find the ways your work contributes to the greater good and how it benefits people.

Reading List

168 Hours: You Have More Time Than You Think, by Laura Vanderkam

Connected: The Surprising Power of Our Social Networks and How They Shape Our Lives, by Nicholas A. Christakis and James H. Fowler

How to Fail at Almost Everything and Still Win Big: Kind of the Story of My Life, by Scott Adams

Mindset: The New Psychology of Success, by Carol S. Dweck

No Sweat: How the Simple Science of Motivation Can Bring You a Lifetime of Fitness, by Michelle Segar

The Best Place to Work: The Art and Science of Creating an Extraordinary Workplace, by Ron Friedman

The Checklist Manifesto: How to Get Things Right, by Atul Gawande

The Last Mile: Creating Social and Economic Value from Behavioral Insights, by Dilip Soman

The Life-Changing Magic of Tidying Up: The Japanese Art of Decluttering and Organizing, by Marie Kondo

The Power of Having Fun: How Meaningful Breaks Help You Get More Done, by Dave Crenshaw

The Power of Habit: Why We Do What We Do in Life and Business, by Charles Duhigg

Tools of Titans: The Tactics, Routines, and Habits of Billionaires, Icons, and World-Class Performers, by Tim Ferriss

Willpower: Rediscovering the Greatest Human Strength, by Roy F. Baumeister and John Tierney

Acknowledgments

There are many people to thank for making this book possible and helping me throughout my life to become the best version of myself:

First and foremost, thank you to my parents Steve and Susan, for bringing me into existence and providing me with the best life possible. Next, my siblings Ken and Jen, for putting up with my eccentric ways for so long, but being good sports about it.

Thanks to the rest of my supportive family: grandparents (Dolores, Bob, Irwin, Dorothy), uncles (Bob, Rick, Tom), aunts (Cathy, Nancy), and cousins (Ricky, Nicole).

All of my amazing friends over the years, including Justin W., Paul W., Matt K., Victor C., Anthony C., Todd G., Chris K., Michael P., Will R., Andrew F., Anthony O., Matt D., and anyone else I've missed: Thank you.

Also, a big thank you to everyone who has supported my work and The Emotion Machine over the past decade, especially to those who I have connected with on Twitter, Facebook, Reddit, email, etc. Your feedback is always listened to and greatly appreciated. It made a big impact on the work done in this book.

Last but not least, thanks to everyone else, including the people at Ulysses Press.

Thank you all!

About the Author

Steven Handel is a 30-year-old psychology author, blogger, and coach. He has been studying psychology and self-improvement for over a decade. In June 2009, he started the popular website *TheEmotionMachine.com*, which currently has over 800 articles covering a wide range of topics including positive psychology, cognitive-behavioral therapy, meditation and mindfulness, behavioral economics, industrial-organizational psychology, emotional intelligence, neuroscience, humanistic psychology, and philosophy.

Steven grew up in Long Island, New York, and studied psychology at Binghamton University. He spent a couple years working at a music and arts venue in Brooklyn, NY, and currently resides in St. Petersburg, Florida. In his free time, Steven can be found going to local music shows, making electronic music, walking his Yorkie, Tila, and watching The Mets.